# Teaching

# Tactics

## HARVESTIME INTERNATIONAL INSTITUTE

This course is part of the **Harvestime International Institute**, a program designed to equip believers for effective spiritual harvest.

The basic theme of the training is to teach what Jesus taught, that which took men who were fishermen, tax collectors, etc., and changed them into reproductive Christians who reached their world with the Gospel in a demonstration of power.

This manual is a single course in one of several modules of curriculum which moves believers from visualizing through deputizing, multiplying, organizing, and mobilizing to achieve the goal of evangelizing.

For further information on additional courses write:

**HARVESTIME INT. NETWORK**
**1110 N. COVENTRY AVE.**
**CLOVIS, CA 93611**

# TABLE OF CONTENTS

# HOW TO USE THIS MANUAL

## MANUAL FORMAT

Each lesson consists of:

**Objectives**: These are the goals you should achieve by studying the chapter. Read them before starting the lesson.

**Key Verse**: This verse emphasizes the main concept of the chapter. Memorize it.

**Chapter Content**: Study each section. Use your Bible to look up any references not printed in the manual.

**Self-Test**: Take this test after you finish studying the chapter. Try to answer the questions without using your Bible or this manual. When you have concluded the Self-Test, check your answers in the answer section provided at the end of the book.

**For Further Study**: This section will help you continue your study of the Word of God, improve your study skills, and apply what you have learned to your life and ministry.

**Final Examination**: If you are enrolled in this course for credit, you received a final examination along with this course. Upon conclusion of this course, you should complete this examination and return it for grading as instructed.

## ADDITIONAL MATERIALS NEEDED

You will need a King James version of the Bible.

# SUGGESTIONS FOR GROUP STUDY

## FIRST MEETING

**Opening**: Open with prayer and introductions. Get acquainted and register the students.

**Establish Group Procedures**: Determine who will lead the meetings, the time, place, and dates for the sessions.

**Praise And Worship**: Invite the presence of the Holy Spirit into your training session.

**Distribute Manuals To Students**: Introduce the manual title, format, and course objectives provided in the first few pages of the manual.

**Make The First Assignment**: Students will read the chapters assigned and take the Self-Tests prior to the next meeting. The number of chapters you cover per meeting will depend on chapter length, content, and the abilities of your group.

## SECOND AND FOLLOWING MEETINGS

**Opening**: Pray. Welcome and register any new students and give them a manual. Take attendance. Have a time of praise and worship.

**Review**: Present a brief summary of what you studied at the last meeting.

**Lesson**: Discuss each section of the chapter using the **HEADINGS IN CAPITAL BOLD FACED LETTERS** as a teaching outline. Ask students for questions or comments on what they have studied. Apply the lesson to the lives and ministries of your students.

**Self-Test**: Review the Self-Tests students have completed. (Note: If you do not want the students to have access to the answers to the Self-Tests, you may remove the answer pages from the back of each manual.)

**For Further Study**: You may do these projects on a group or individual basis.

**Final Examination**: If your group is enrolled in this course for credit, you received a final examination with this course. Reproduce a copy for each student and administer the exam upon conclusion of this course.

# INTRODUCTION

The subject of this course is *"Teaching Tactics."* "Teaching" is the act of instructing another person. Biblical teaching includes imparting knowledge and demonstrating how to apply that knowledge to personal life and ministry. "Tactics" are methods used to achieve a goal, purpose, or objective. In the military, the subject of "tactics" teaches soldiers how to use their weapons to achieve an advantage over the enemy. The same is true in the spiritual world. If we apply God's methods or "tactics," we can conquer spiritual enemies which include the world, the flesh and Satan with all his powers.

In *"Teaching Tactics"* you will learn how to use a great spiritual weapon. That weapon is the sword of the Spirit which is the Word of God (Ephesians 6:17). You will learn tactics of preaching and teaching God's Word for the purpose of defeating the enemy. This course uses God's Word, the Holy Bible, as the revelation upon which all teaching is based. In Biblical teaching the teacher, subject, and methods must all be in harmony with the Bible.

Teaching is not just the communicating of doctrine or information. Students must experience God, not just learn information about Him. Teaching is the transmission [imparting] of both a life and lifestyle. The <u>life</u> to be imparted to students is new life in Jesus Christ through new birth spiritually (John 3). The <u>lifestyle</u> to be imparted is that of the Kingdom of God. Students must be taught how to live as "citizens" in this Kingdom, learning both the privileges and responsibilities of their position.

Sometimes, we have been content to borrow man-made educational systems instead of learning and applying what God's Word reveals about teaching. This course focuses on the Biblical message and methods of teaching. You will learn and apply methods of the master teacher, Jesus Christ. You will understand the functions of God the Father, the Son, and the Holy Spirit in your teaching.

Guidelines are given for analyzing the audience, stating objectives, planning the lesson, using different teaching methods, and evaluating your teaching. The relationship between teaching and preaching is examined and guidelines are given for preaching Biblical messages. You will also learn how to train others to teach and how to adapt your teaching to illiterate people [those who cannot read or write].

If you are taking Harvestime International Institute courses in their suggested order, this is the second course of the Module entitled "Multiplying," a module which details how to multiply by sharing with others the spiritual truths you have learned. Other courses in the Module include *"Biblical World View," "Multiplication Methodologies,"* and *"Power Principles."*

# COURSE OBJECTIVES

Upon completion of this course you will be able to:

- Explain the difference between the position of a teacher, the gift of teaching, and the command to all believers to teach.
- Summarize the mission and methods of the master teacher, Jesus Christ.
- Explain the functions of the Father, Son, and Holy Spirit in teaching.
- Use Biblical methods of teaching.
- Explain the mission of the teacher.
- List Biblical qualifications for teachers.
- Analyze the audience.
- State instructional objectives.
- Teach a Bible lesson.
- Explain the relationship between teaching and preaching.
- Preach a Bible message.
- Develop and use audio-visual aids.
- Evaluate your teaching and preaching.
- Train others to teach.
- Select and/or develop Biblical curriculum.
- Adapt your teaching to those who are illiterate.

# CHAPTER ONE

## AN INTRODUCTION TO TEACHING

**OBJECTIVES:**

Upon completion of this chapter you will be able to:

- Identify a New Testament reference that commissions believers to teach.
- Define the words "teach," "teacher," and "teaching."
- Explain why we need teachers.
- Explain the difference between the leadership position of teacher and the speaking gift of teaching.
- Identify who is to be taught.
- Identify two main objectives of teaching.
- List Biblical warnings given to teachers.

**KEY VERSES:**

**Go ye therefore, and teach all nations, baptizing them in the name of the Father, and of the Son and of the Holy Ghost:**

**Teaching them to observe all things whatsoever I have commanded you: and, lo, I am with you alway, even unto the end of the world. (Matthew 28:19-20)**

### INTRODUCTION

Have you ever explained to another person something they did not know? Perhaps you showed them how to do a certain task? If so, you have already experienced teaching.

You may be asking yourself, "Why should I study this lesson? Why should I take a course on `teaching tactics'?" In this chapter you will learn <u>why</u> each believer must know how to teach. You will learn what it means to teach, the main objectives of teaching, why teachers are needed, and who is to be taught.

You will learn the difference between the leadership position of a teacher, the gift of teaching, and the general command to all believers to teach. You will also learn the serious responsibility of teaching as you study special Biblical warnings.

# THE COMMISSION TO TEACH

From the beginning of Biblical history, God commanded His people to teach His Word:

> **And these words, which I command thee this day, shall be in thine heart:**
>
> **And thou shalt teach them diligently unto thy children, and shalt talk of them when thou sittest in thine house, and when thou walkest by the way, and when thou liest down, and when thou risest up. (Deuteronomy 6:6-7)**

The teaching of God's Word was the responsibility of every believer in Old Testament times.

After His death and resurrection and before returning to Heaven, Jesus Christ gave His followers some important instructions:

> **Go ye therefore, and teach all nations, baptizing them in the name of the Father, and of the Son and of the Holy Ghost:**
>
> **Teaching them to observe all things whatsoever I have commanded you: and, lo, I am with you alway, even unto the end of the world. (Matthew 28:19-20)**

Each follower of Jesus was to teach "all nations." They were to lead people to repentance and baptism in Christ and then continue to instruct them in "all things" Jesus had taught.

All those who serve the Lord are to be "apt" or "able" to teach others:

> **And the servant of the Lord must be...apt to teach...(II Timothy 2:24)**

All mature believers should be involved in teaching others. Paul corrected some believers because they were spiritually immature and could not teach:

> **For when for the time ye ought to be teachers, ye have need that one teach you again which be the first principles of the oracles of God; and are become such as have need of milk, and not of strong meat. (Hebrews 5:12)**

These believers had not grown spiritually so they could teach others. They were still in need of basic teaching [the milk of the Word] themselves. Every believer is to teach. This is why the subject of teaching is of concern to all Christians.

4

# DEFINITION OF TEACHING

The word "teach" means to instruct, show, demonstrate, inform, impart knowledge, train and guide the studies of another. A "teacher" is one who teaches. "Teaching" is the act of instructing and training others.

## WHY DO WE NEED TEACHERS?

Teaching and preaching by true believers are the methods God has chosen to reach the nations with the Gospel. Read the story of the Ethiopian eunuch [leader] in Acts 8:26-40. This man was at the right spiritual place. He was in Jerusalem where the great temple of worship was located (Acts 8:27). He was there for the right purpose. He had come to worship (Acts 8:27). He was reading the right book. He was reading a portion of God's Word in Isaiah 53:7 (Acts 8:30). But he still needed someone to help Him understand. He needed a teacher. God sent Philip to instruct him. The eunuch accepted the Gospel and was baptized in water.

Without teachers, unsaved people are like sheep without a shepherd. They do not understand which way to go:

> **And Jesus, when He came out, saw much people, and was moved with compassion toward them, because they were as sheep not having a shepherd; and He began to teach them many things. (Mark 6:34)**

Even believers have problems without proper teaching. God said...

> **MY PEOPLE are destroyed for lack of knowledge...(Hosea 4:6)**

## THE MAIN OBJECTIVES

There are two main objectives of Biblical preaching and teaching: Evangelism and discipleship. God uses believers who are part of His Church to accomplish these objectives.

The Church is a group of people who have heard and responded to the call of God and are united by faith in Jesus Christ. It is made up of all true believers who have repented from sin and accepted Jesus as Savior.

The local Church is a group of believers who have organized in a certain area to accomplish the purposes of God in that community. Each local Church is part of what the New Testament calls the Body of Christ. The Body of Christ is the Church which is composed of believers of all ages and times in all parts of the world.

The Church is called the Body of Christ because it is the means through which God accomplishes His purposes in the world today. Jesus is the head of the Church. Believers are

His body, carrying out God's purposes in the earth.

The main purpose of God in the earth is described in the book of Ephesians:

>**...According to His good pleasure which He hath purposed in Himself:**
>
>**That in the dispensation of the fullness of times He might gather together in one all things in Christ...(Ephesians 1:9-10)**
>
>**In whom we have redemption through His blood, the forgiveness of sins, according to the riches of His grace.  (Ephesians 1:7)**

God's purpose is that every person be brought into a personal relationship with Himself through Jesus.  His method of accomplishing this purpose is to use the Church:

>**To the intent that now unto the principalities and powers  in heavenly places, might be known by the Church the manifold wisdom of God,**
>
>**According to the eternal purpose which He purposed in Christ Jesus our Lord...  (Ephesians 3:10-11)**

Each believer is to share the Gospel of Jesus Christ and lead others to a right relationship with God. This is called "evangelism."

But read the key verse of this lesson again:

>**Go ye therefore, and teach all nations, baptizing them in the name of the Father, and of the Son and of the Holy Ghost:**
>
>**Teaching them to observe all things whatsoever I have commanded you: and, lo, I am with you alway, even unto the end of the world. (Matthew 28:19-20)**

After accepting the Gospel message, new believers must be taught "all things" Jesus commanded.  They must learn how to live in the new Kingdom of God of which they are now a part.  This kind of teaching is called "discipleship."  Evangelism and discipleship are the main objectives of Biblical teaching and preaching.

## WHO DO WE TEACH?

We teach two main groups of people:

6

## ALL NATIONS:

We must teach unbelievers. Every person in every nation is to hear the Gospel. We accomplish this through teaching and preaching God's Word:

> **Go ye therefore, and teach all nations, baptizing them in the name of the Father, and of the Son and of the Holy Ghost. (Matthew 28:19)**

## FAITHFUL MEN:

We are also to teach "faithful" men and women who become believers in Jesus...

> **Teaching them to observe all things whatsoever I have commanded you: and, lo, I am with you alway, even unto the end of the world. (Matthew 28:20)**

These people are to continue the process by teaching others:

> **And the things that thou hast heard of me among many witnesses, the same commit thou to faithful men, who shall be able to teach others also. (II Timothy 2:2)**

Each person taught is to teach others who are also able to teach. This is the pattern of continuous teaching that rapidly multiplies to spread the Gospel throughout the world:

> **Let him that is taught in the Word communicate unto him that teacheth in all good things. (Galatians 6:6)**

## TYPES OF TEACHERS

In the world there are many types of teachers. There are teachers in public schools at every level, from childhood through college age. For every job there are teachers who can teach others to perform that special task or service. But when we speak of teachers in this course, we are not talking about teachers in the world system of education. We are speaking of teachers God sets in the Church and of the teaching task of believers.

You have already learned that all believers are to teach others the Gospel [evangelism] and teach new believers [discipleship]. In addition to this general commission to teach, God gives some believers special gifts of teaching:

> **And God hath set some in the church, first apostles, secondarily prophets, thirdly teachers...(I Corinthians 12:28)**

**And He gave some...teachers...   (Ephesians 4:11)**

There are many special abilities God gives which are called "spiritual gifts." These abilities enable believers to accomplish God's purposes in ministry.   There are two spiritual gifts of teaching.   There is a leadership position of teacher and a speaking gift of teaching.   Those with these gifts have a special ability of communicating God's Word effectively in such a way that others learn and apply what is taught. Their teaching ability goes beyond that which every believer should have for evangelism and discipleship.   They have  an anointing and feel a "call" or urge to teach and preach God's Word.

God sets some of these teachers in leadership positions to guide the affairs of the church.   Acts 13:1-4  illustrates the leadership position of teaching.   Others are especially anointed of God to teach, but do not hold a leadership position in the Church. They only teach, they do not guide the affairs of the church.

Not everyone has the leadership position of teacher.   Not everyone has the spiritual gift of teaching.   Paul wrote:

> **Are all apostles?  Are all prophets?  Are all teachers?...**
> **(I Corinthians 12:29)**

The answer to these questions are "No."  Not everyone has these spiritual gifts.  The Body of Christ is similar to the human body.  Each person has a different position just as each member of your body has a different function:

> **For as we have many members in one body, and all members have not the**
> **same office:**
>
> **So we, being many, are one body in Christ, and every one members one of**
> **another.**
>
> **Having then gifts differing according to the grace that is given to us...let us**
> **wait on our ministering...he that teacheth, on teaching.  (Romans 12:4-7)**

It is important to discover your spiritual gift because when the whole Body is working properly with each person in his place, God's purposes are accomplished:

> **From whom the whole body fitly joined together and compacted by that**
> **which every joint supplieth, according to the effectual working in the**
> **measure of every part, maketh increase of the body unto the edifying of**
> **itself in love.  (Ephesians 4:16)**

But remember: Even if you do not have these special gifts of teaching, God has called ALL believers to teach the Gospel to all nations in evangelism and to train new believers in the discipleship process.

## WHAT DO WE TEACH?

The Word of God is the authority on which all Biblical teaching is based. The total revelation of God's Word must be taught. When you teach God's Word you must not just teach doctrine or factual information. You must communicate a life and a lifestyle. You communicate the life of Jesus and seek to bring all men into fellowship with Him. You teach the lifestyle of the Kingdom of God of which new believers become a part. Other books and materials may be used in teaching, but they should always be in harmony with God's Word.

Later in this course you will study in more detail the content of Biblical teaching as you learn what Jesus taught and what the early Church leaders continued to teach after He returned to Heaven.

## WORDS OF WARNING

There are three Biblical warnings God gives about teaching:

## TEACHING MUST BE BASED ON GOD'S WORD, NOT DOCTRINES OF MEN:

> **Howbeit in vain do they worship me, teaching for doctrines the commandments of men. (Mark 7:7)**

Teaching man's rules, commandments, and doctrines is "vain." This means it is unsuccessful and accomplishes no good purpose. Biblical teaching is not based on the wisdom of man:

> **Which things also we speak, not in the word which man's wisdom teacheth, but which the Holy Ghost teacheth; comparing spiritual things with spiritual. (I Corinthians 2:13)**

God's wisdom accomplishes His purposes in the lives of those taught:

> **...Christ in you, the hope of glory;**

> **Whom we preach, warning every man, and teaching every man in all wisdom; that we may present every man perfect in Christ Jesus. (Colossians 1:27-28)**

9

## TEACHERS MUST LIVE WHAT THEY TEACH:

> Thou therefore which teachest another, teachest thou not thyself? Thou that preachest a man should not steal, dost thou steal?
>
> Thou that sayest a man should not commit adultery, dost thou commit adultery? Thou that abhorrest idols, dost thou commit sacrilege? (Romans 2:21-22) (See also Matthew 5:19)

Teachers must live what they teach because they will be judged on the basis of what they have taught:

> My brethren, be not many masters [teachers], knowing that we shall receive the greater condemnation. (James 3:1)

Teachers must have experiential knowledge of God's Word. This means they must understand through experience [not just head knowledge] what they are teaching. Paul speaks of those who...

> Desiring to be teachers of the law; understand neither what they say, nor whereof they affirm. (I Timothy 1:7)

Understanding comes through experience and application of God's Word in your own life.

## THERE WILL BE FALSE TEACHERS:

> But there were false prophets also among the people, even as there shall be false teachers among you, who privily shall bring in damnable heresies, even denying the Lord that bought them, and bring upon themselves swift destruction. (II Peter 2:1)

Some of these false teachers will attract big crowds because they say what people want to hear:

> For the time will come when they will not endure sound doctrine; but after their own lusts shall they heap to themselves teachers, having itching ears:
>
> And they shall turn away their ears from the truth and shall be turned unto fables. (II Timothy 4:3-4)

Many false teachers will have a wrong motive. They will teach for financial gain:

> Whose mouths must be stopped, who subvert whole houses, teaching things which they ought not for filthy lucre's sake. (Titus 1:11)

10

You must not accept the doctrines of false teachers:

> **But though <u>we</u>, or <u>an angel</u> from Heaven, preach any other Gospel unto you than that which we have preached unto you, let him be accursed.**
>
> **As we said before, so say I now again, if any <u>man</u> preach any other Gospel unto you than that ye have received, let him be accursed. (Galatians 1:8-9)**

# SELF-TEST

1. Write the Key Verses from memory.

_____

_____

2. List a New Testament reference that commissions believers to teach _____

3. Define these words:

Teach:_____

Teacher:_____

Teaching:_____

4. Why do we need teachers?

_____

5. Explain the difference between the leadership position of teacher and the gift of teaching.

_____

6. Is this statement true or false?  "All believers do not have the gift or leadership position of teaching, but all believers are to teach."  The statement is_____.

7. Who are we to teach?_____

8. What are the two main objectives of Biblical teaching?

_____  and  _____

9. List three  Biblical  warnings  about teaching discussed in this lesson.

_____     _____

_____

(Answers to self-tests are provided at the conclusion of the final chapter in this manual.)

# FOR FURTHER STUDY

1. II Peter chapter 2 and the book of Jude list some of the personal characteristics by which we can recognize false teachers.

2. If you do not know what spiritual gift God has given you, obtain the Harvestime International Institute course, *"Ministry of the Holy Spirit."* It will help you discover your spiritual gift.

3. The Harvestime International Institute course, *"Leaven-Like Evangelism,"* explains how to evangelize in such a manner that spiritual reproduction will continue, even as leaven spreads through a loaf of bread.

4. The Harvestime International Institute course entitled *"Multiplication Methodologies"* details how to disciple new believers.

5. Study the following examples of teachers in the New Testament. Who do you think might have had the leadership position of teacher? Who might have had only the speaking gift of teaching?

| | |
|---|---|
| -Appollos: | Acts 18:24-25 |
| -Aquilla and Priscilla: | Acts 18:26 |
| -Paul: | Acts 20:20-21,27; 21:28 |
| -Unnamed: | Acts 13:1 |
| -Peter: | Acts 5:28-29 |

6. In this lesson you learned that from the beginning of Biblical history God instructed His people to teach His Word. Continue your study of the subject of teaching in the Old Testament by reading the following references in your Bible:

Deuteronomy 4:9,10,14; 6:9,20; 5:31; 11:19; 17:11; 20:18; 24:8; 31:19; 33:10
Exodus 4:12,15; 18:20; 24:12; 35:34
Leviticus 10:11; 14:57
Psalms 119:99
Proverbs 9:9; 16:23
Micah 3:11
II Chronicles 17:7
Ezra 7:10
Judges 3:2; 13:8
I Samuel 12:23
II Samuel 1:18
I Kings 8:36
II Kings 17:27

7. Here are some things <u>God</u> wants to teach us:

Psalms 18:34; 25:4-12; 27:11; 32:8; 34:11; 45:4; 51:13; 71:17; 86:11; 90:12; 94:10,12; 105:22; 119:12,68,99,102,104,124,135,171; 143:10; 144:1
II Samuel 22:35
Isaiah 2:3; 28:9,26; 48:17
I Chronicles 25:7
Micah 4:2

8. Study these verses on instruction:

Psalms 2:10
Proverbs 5:13; 1:2-8; 4:1,13; 6:23; 8:10,33;  9:9; 10:17; 12:1; 13:1; 15:33; 19:20,27; 21:11; 23:12,23; 24:32
Isaiah 8:11
Luke 1:4
Romans 2:18
Philippians 4:12
II Timothy 3:16

9. There are serious results for refusing Godly instruction.  Study the following verses:

Proverbs 1:7; 5:12,13,23; 13:18; 15:5,32; 16:22
Jeremiah 17:23; 32:33
Psalms 50:17

# CHAPTER TWO

## A TEACHER COME FROM GOD:  THE MISSION

**OBJECTIVES:**

Upon completion of this chapter you will be able to:

- Explain the functions of the Father, Son, and Holy Spirit in teaching.
- Identify Jesus Christ as the greatest teacher, the example for all to follow.
- Identify personality qualities that should be evident in the life of a teacher.
- Explain the mission of Jesus as a teacher come from God.
- Summarize where, when, and who Jesus taught.
- Give a Biblical reference which confirms we are sent by Jesus as He was sent by God.
- Identify your mission as a teacher come from God.

**KEY VERSE:**

> **The same came to Jesus by night, and said unto Him, Rabbi, we know that thou art <u>a teacher come from God</u>:  for no man can do these miracles that thou doest, except God be with Him.  (John 3:2)**

## INTRODUCTION

In this chapter you will learn the functions of the Father, Son, and Holy Spirit in Biblical teaching.  You will learn details of the mission of Jesus, "a teacher come from God."  From this study you will discover the divine purpose of your own mission as a teacher.

## DIVINE AGENTS IN TEACHING

Biblical teaching is empowered by divine agents. This means there are spiritual powers behind such teaching.  It is not just the teaching of a man.  The divine agents of Biblical teaching are God the Father, the Son Jesus Christ, and the Holy Spirit.

**GOD THE FATHER:**

You learned in the last chapter that it is God who sets believers in the Church with the spiritual gift and office of teaching (Ephesians 4:11).  In Biblical teaching the subject that is taught

God's Word. You will learn more about this in the next chapter as you study the message of the teacher come from God.

It is God the Father who sent Jesus Christ to earth to teach us about Himself and to provide salvation for all mankind:

> **For God so loved the world, that He gave His only begotten Son, that whosoever believeth in Him should not perish, but have everlasting life.**

> **For God sent not His Son into the world to condemn the world; but that the world through Him might be saved.  (John 3:16-17)**

## JESUS CHRIST:

Jesus Christ, God's Son, is the greatest spiritual teacher of all times.  Jesus was sent to earth by God the Father:

> **The same came to Jesus by night, and said unto Him, Rabbi, we know that thou art <u>a teacher come from God</u>:  for no man can do these miracles that thou doest, except God be with Him.  (John 3:2)**

Since Jesus was sent to earth as a teacher representing God, He is the example for Biblical teachers to follow.   Jesus is the one who sends believers to the world as teachers:

> **As my Father hath sent me, even so send I you. (John 20:21)**

> **And Jesus came and spake unto them, saying, All power is given unto me in Heaven and in earth.**

> **<u>Go ye therefore, and teach</u> all nations, baptizing them in the name of the Father, and of the Son, and of the Holy Ghost;**

> **<u>Teaching</u> them to observe all things whatsoever I have commanded you: and, lo, I am with you alway, even unto the end of the world. (Matthew 28:18-20)**

## THE HOLY SPIRIT:

When Jesus returned to Heaven following His death and resurrection, the Holy Spirit was sent by God to be the resident teacher in believers.   The Holy Spirit dwells within your spirit and teaches you the things of God:

> **But the Comforter, which is the Holy Ghost, whom the Father will send in**

**my name, He shall teach you all things, and bring all things to your remembrance whatsoever I have said unto you. (John 14:26)**

Additional functions of the Holy Spirit in teaching are revealed in the following passages. The Holy Spirit:

1. Gives instruction in "all things" Jesus taught (John 14:26).
2. Helps you remember what you learn (John 14:26).
3. Guides you into all truth (John 16:13).
4. Declares [announces] future events in God's plan (John 16:13).
5. Reveals the "deep things" of God (I Corinthians 2:10).
6. Is the wisdom behind Biblical teaching (I Corinthians 2:13).
7. Teaches you what to say in crisis situations (Luke 12:12).
8. Anoints you to teach and minister (Luke 4:18, I John 2:27).
9. Enables prayer for students (Romans 8:26).

The Holy Spirit is also at work in the lives of those you teach:

1. As you teach, the Holy Ghost is the spiritual power that convicts sinners and causes them to respond to the Gospel message (John 16:7-11).
2. The Holy Spirit reveals the Lord Jesus Christ to them (John 16:14).
3. The Holy Spirit leads them into the "born again" experience (John 3:5,6,8).
4. He will lead them to life in the Spirit instead of the flesh (Galatians 5:16).
5. He will witness to their hearts the truths of God's Word (Acts 5:29-32).

## THE MASTER TEACHER

Jesus is the example for Christian teachers to follow. He is the model for Biblical teaching. Because of this, it is important to learn all you can about Him as a teacher. First, let us look at qualities in the life of Jesus that should be evident in the lives of Christian teachers:

## FRUIT OF THE HOLY SPIRIT:

The "fruit" of the Holy Spirit was evident in the life of Jesus. Spiritual "fruit" refers to the positive qualities the Holy Spirit wants to develop in the lives of all believers:

**...The fruit of the Spirit is love, joy, peace, longsuffering, gentleness, goodness, faith,**

**Meekness, temperance; against such there is no law. (Galatians 5:22-23)**

Read through the books of Matthew, Mark, Luke, and John and note how each of these qualities were evident in the life of Jesus. Each Spirit-filled teacher of God's Word should also have these same qualities. It is spiritual fruit, not gifts, that are the true test of ministry:

**And all the people were amazed, and said, Is not this the son of David? (Matthew 12:33)**

## ATTITUDES OF JESUS:

In addition to spiritual fruit, Jesus also was a model of proper attitudes that should be evident in the lives of teachers of God's Word. The following Scriptures illustrate these attitudes:

-Jesus had great compassion for people and their needs: Matthew 15:32; Mark 1:32-35; 8:2-3; Luke 10:54-56; 19:41

-This compassion led Him to intercession for those He taught: Matthew 11:21-24; 23:37-39

-This resulted in concern for the Father's business: Luke 2:49; 4:43; John 4:34; 9:4

-Jesus had an attitude of no condemnation towards those He taught: (Mark 2:17; John 8:1-11). He accepted people where they were and then led them to the level of faith where they should be. He did not condemn Thomas when He doubted (John 20:24-29). He did not condemn the ruler who felt it necessary that Jesus come to his house to pray for his daughter (Matthew 9:18-26) although it had already been shown this was not necessary (Matthew 8:5-13).

-Although Jesus did not condemn, He was uncompromising with sin. This means He did not in any way approve of it or overlook it: Matthew 11:21-24; 15:3-9; 12:12-13; Mark 10:17; Luke 5:31-32; 19:45-46

-Jesus demonstrated a trust in God for the impossible: Mark 10:17; 11:22-24; Luke 18:27

-He demonstrated boldness and authority in His teaching: Matthew 21:23-27; Mark 8:38; 11:24-33; Luke 5:24

-Most important, He had a servant's attitude toward those to whom He ministered: Matthew 20:25-28; 23:2-12; Mark 10:42-45; Luke 22:25-27

## THE MISSION OF THE MASTER

When we speak of the "mission" of Jesus, we refer to the following:

> Why Jesus taught.
> When and where He taught.
> Who He taught.

<u>What</u> He taught.
<u>How</u> He taught.

Let us examine why, when, where, and who Jesus taught. Following chapters will focus on the message [what] and methods [how] of His mission.

## <u>WHY HE TAUGHT</u>:

Jesus taught because He was commissioned by God to do so. The mission [reason or purpose] of Jesus is summarized in the following Scriptures:

> **Think not that I am come to destroy the law or the prophets; I am not come to destroy, but to fulfill. (Matthew 5:17)**

> **I am not come to call the righteous, but sinners to repentance. (Matthew 9:13)**

> **Think not that I am come to send peace on the earth: I come not to send peace, but a sword. (Matthew 10:34)**

(Jesus meant His message would cause division; some would accept it and some would not.)

> **I am not sent but unto the lost sheep of the house of Israel. (Matthew 15:24)**

> **For the Son of Man is come to save that which is lost. (Matthew 18:11) (See also Luke 19:10).**

> **I came not to call the righteous, but sinners to repentance. (Mark 2:17)**

> **Let us go into the next towns, that I may preach there also; for therefore I came forth. (Mark 1:38)**

> **For the Son of man is not come to destroy men's lives, but to save them... (Luke 9:56)**

> **And said unto them, Thus it is written, and thus it behooved Christ to suffer, and to rise from the dead the third day:**

> **And that repentance and remission of sins should be preached in His name among all nations, beginning at Jerusalem.**

> **And ye are witnesses of these things. (Luke 24:46-48)**

Jesus saith unto them, My meat is to do the will of Him that sent me, and to finish His work.  (John 4:34)

For I came down from Heaven not to do mine own will, but the will of Him that sent me.  (John 6:38)

...To this end was I born, and for this cause came I into the world, that I should bear witness unto the truth...  (John 18:37)

I am come a light unto the world, that whosoever believeth  on  me should not abide in darkness.   (John 12:46)

I speak that which I have seen with my Father...(John 9:38)

 ...I am come that they might have life, and that they might have it more abundantly.  (John 10:10)

## WHEN AND WHERE HE TAUGHT:

Jesus taught on the Sabbath Day:

> And they went into Capernaum; and straightway on the Sabbath  day He entered into the synagogue, and taught. (Mark 1:21)
> (See also Luke 4:31; 6:6; 13:10).

Jesus taught daily:

> And He taught daily in the temple...  (Luke 19:47)

He taught in cities and villages:

> Let us go into the next towns, that I may preach there also; for therefore I came forth.  (Mark 1:38)

> And Jesus went about all the cities and villages teaching...
> (Matthew 9:35)  (See also Matthew 11:1; Mark 1:38; 6:6; Luke 13:22).

He taught in the centers of religious worship:

> And Jesus went about all Galilee, teaching in  their synagogues...  (Matthew 4:23) (See also  Matthew 13:54;  Mark 1:21; 6:2; Luke 4:15; 6:6; 13:10; John 6:59; 18:20).

And when He was come into the <u>temple</u>, the chief priests and the elders of the people came unto Him as He was teaching... (Matthew 21:23) (See also Matthew 26:55; Mark 12:35; 14:49; Luke 19:47; 20:21; 21:37; John 7:14,28; 8:2,20).

<u>He taught anywhere and everywhere</u>:

And He went forth again by the sea side; and all the multitude resorted unto Him, and He taught them. (Mark 2:13) (See also Mark 4:1; 10:1; Luke 5:3).

## WHO HE TAUGHT:

<u>Jesus taught crowds of people</u>:

And seeing the multitudes, He went up into a mountain... And He opened His mouth and taught them, saying... (Matthew 5:1-2)

(See the "For Further Study" section of this chapter for additional references on the ministry of Jesus to crowds).

<u>Jesus taught individuals</u>:

See John 3 and 4 and the "For Further Study" section of this chapter for references on the ministry of Jesus to individuals.

<u>Jesus taught men and women in all levels of society</u>:

-He taught the rich: Mark 10:17-22

-He taught the poor: Luke 4:18

-He taught all levels of society: The Samaritan woman was of a lower class (John 4). Nicodemus was a ruler and a member of the upper class (John 3).

-He taught those of His own race:

I am not sent but unto the lost sheep of the house of Israel. (Matthew 15:24)

...teaching throughout all Jewry, beginning from Galilee to this place. (Luke 23:5)

-He taught those of other races.  See John 4 where Jesus taught the Samaritan woman.

-He taught religious leaders:

> **And it came to pass on a certain day, as He was teaching, that there were Pharisees and doctors of the law sitting by, which were come out of every town of Galilee, and Judaea, and Jerusalem; and the power of the Lord was present to heal them.  (Luke 5:17)**

-He taught all ages:  He taught young rulers (Mark 10:17-22) and a man who had waited 38 years for a miracle (John 5:1-16).

-His teaching mission was to the whole world, people from every culture, tribe, and tongue:

> **And He said unto them, I must preach the Kingdom of God to  other  cities also: for therefore am I sent.  (Luke 4:43)**

Jesus gave special teaching to His disciples:

> **And He thought them many things by parables, and said unto them in His doctrine.  (Mark 4:2)**

> **Then Jesus sent the multitude away, and went into the house:  and His disciples came unto Him, saying, Declare unto us the parable of the tares of the field.  (Matthew 13:36)**

Jesus taught special lessons to His disciples because they were the men He was training for leadership in the Church.

Sometimes Jesus combined groups and taught them together:  See Luke 15:1-17:11.

## "SO SEND I YOU"

Jesus made an important statement concerning His followers which applies to all true believers.  He said...

> **As my Father hath sent me, even so send I you. (John 20:21)**

This means believers are sent into the world with the same mission as Jesus.  Like Jesus, we are teachers "come from God."  We can briefly summarize our mission in teaching by this statement:  As the Father sent Jesus, so are we sent to accomplish similar purposes.  His mission is our mission.  Since we have the same mission as Jesus, we should follow His example in who, where, and when we teach.  Our mission is to all people, anywhere, anytime.

# SELF-TEST

1. Write the Key Verse from memory.

_____

_____

2. What is the function of God the Father in teaching?

_____

_____

3. What is the function of Jesus Christ in teaching?

_____

_____

4. What are the functions of the Holy Spirit in teaching?

_____

_____

_____

5. Fill in these blanks with the correct words.

_____ _____ was the master teacher, the example for all to follow.

6. List some of the positive personality qualities which should be developed in the life of a teacher.

_____

_____

7.  Summarize the mission of Jesus as a teacher come from God.

_____

_____

_____

8.  Write a brief summary on each of the following topics.  During His earthly ministry...

Where did Jesus teach?

_____

When did Jesus teach?

_____

Who did Jesus teach?

_____

9.  What Biblical reference confirms we are sent by Jesus as He was by God?

_____

10. Briefly summarize your mission as a teacher come from God.

_____

_____

_____

_____

(Answers to self-tests are provided at the conclusion of the final chapter in this manual.)

# FOR FURTHER STUDY

1. Study the following references for further study on the ministry of Jesus to crowds:

**Matthew:** 5:1-2; 7:28-29; 8:1-2 [individual in midst of multitude]; 8:16-17,34; 9:1-8,36-38; 11:7; 13:1-9; 14:13-23; 15:30-39; 17:14; 19:2; 20:29-34; 21:8-11; 22:23; 26:47

**Mark:** 1:33-35,45; 2:1-5,7-15,20-21,32-35; 4:1-36; 5:14-17,21-43; 6:2-5,33-46,55-56; 7:24,31-37; 8:1-9; 9:14-27; 10:1,46-52; 11:8-10; 14:43-52; 15:8

**Luke:** 2:45-52; 4:16-30,40-44; 5:1,15-16,18-26; 6:17-7:1; 7:11-18; 8:1,37,40,56; 9:12-18,37; 12:1; 13:11-17; 18:35-43; 19:1-10,36-40; 22:47; 23:1

**John:** 2:1-11; 4:39-42; 5:1,13; 6:5-15,22; 7:40; 8:1-9; 12:9,12-13

2. Study the following references for further study on the ministry of Jesus to individuals:

**Matthew:** Chapter 8 (leper, servant, Peter's mother-in-law, a scribe); Chapter 9 (a man sick of palsy, diseased woman, child); 12:9-13 (a man with a withered hand); 12:22 (demon possessed); 15:21-28 (woman with demon-possessed daughter); 17:17-18 (a man with demon-possessed son); 19:16-22 (rich young man); 22:34-40 (a lawyer); 26:6-13 (woman with ointment).

**Mark:** 1:23-26 (man in synagogue with unclean spirit); 1:40-45 (leper); 5:1-20 ("Legion"); 8:22-26 (blind man); 10:46-52 (blind Bartimaeus).

**Luke:** 7:11-17 (dead man); 8:2 (Mary Magdalene); 9:57-62 (individuals who would be disciples); 10:25-37 (a lawyer); 10:38-42 (Martha); 12:13-15 (a brother concerned about inheritance); 13:10-17 (woman with spirit of infirmity); 13:23-30 (unidentified questioner); 14:1-6 (man with dropsy); 19:1-10 (Zacchaeus).

**John:** 1:47-51 (Nathanael); Chapter 3 (Nicodemus); 4:4-42 (Samaritan woman); 5:1-16 (lame man at Bethesda); 8:1-11 (woman caught in adultery); Chapter 9 (man blind from birth); Chapter 11 (Lazarus, Martha); 13:1-10; 21:15-25 (Peter); 19:25-27 (His mother); 20:11-18 (Mary); 20:24-29 (Thomas).

3. Jesus is called "teacher" 48 times in the Gospels. Find and mark these references in your Bible.

4. Harvestime International Institute has a course entitled *"The Ministry Of The Holy*

*Spirit"* which provides further instruction on the importance of the Holy Spirit in life and ministry.

5. You learned in this lesson how Jesus taught at any time and any place. This followed the Old Testament principle of God given in Deuteronomy 6:6-7. Read this passage in your Bible.

6. Study the following charts which add to our understanding of the divine agents behind Biblical teaching:

## The Nature of Revelation
## I Corinthians 2:9-13

| | |
|---|---|
| What no eye has seen, nor ear heard nor the heart of man conceived <u>what God has prepared</u> for those who love Him, | the information is not based on human experience |
| <u>God has revealed to us through the Spirit.</u> The Spirit searches everything, even the depths of God. For what person knows a man's thoughts except the spirit of man which is in him? So also no one <u>comprehends the thoughts</u> of God except the Spirit of God. | purpose of the Holy Spirit in teaching |
| Now we have received not the spirit of the world, but the Spirit which is from God, <u>that we might understand</u> the gifts bestowed on us by God. | the purpose of revelation |
| And we <u>impart this in words</u> not taught by human wisdom but taught by the Spirit, interpreting spiritual truths to those who possess the Spirit. (Revised Standard Version) | revelation is imparted in words taught by the Holy Spirit |

## I Corinthians 2:1 - 4:7

| **Our Part** | **God's Part** |
|---|---|

we come not with great speech or intellect
we emphasize Christ and His cross

we rely not upon human wisdom, but upon. . . . . . . .　the demonstration of the power of the Spirit.

for mature believers we speak spiritual wisdom. . . .　that has been revealed by God

-The Spirit unveils things that never occurred to natural man

-He shares the deepest truths of God

-Only He understands the thoughts of God

-He gives insight into God's grace

we set forth these spiritual truths in words. . . . .　that the Spirit teaches

we appreciate them. . . . . . . . . . . . . .　by spiritual insight
we have the thoughts of Christ

we are mere servants. . . . . . . . . . . . .　to whom the Lord has given a task

some of us plant, some water. . . . . . . . . .　but God gives the growth

we are nothing in ourselves, compared with . . . . .　God who gives the growth

the planter and waterer are one in aim . . . . . .　yet each gets his own reward according to his work

| Our Part | God's Part |
|---|---|
| we are God's fellow workers; you are His field, His house. | according to God's commission |
| one is the architect who lays the foundation (Christ), while another builds upon it. each one must be careful how he builds . . . . . . . | the judgment day will test by fire each man's work; if his work stands the test he will receive his reward |
| we are God's temple . . . . . . . . . . . . | where the Spirit has His permanent home |
| the world's wisdom is foolishness with God; we cannot boast of men  but everything [spiritual] belongs to you in Christ, in God we are servants of Christ and stewards of God's truths, who must prove worthy of the trust . . | our only judge is God Himself who will expose secret motives and give praise accordingly |
|  | all we have is a gift from God which excludes boasting. |

# CHAPTER THREE

## A TEACHER COME FROM GOD:  THE MESSAGE - PART I

**OBJECTIVES:**

Upon completion of this chapter you will be able to:

- Summarize the basic message taught by Jesus Christ.
- Give  a Biblical reference which summarizes basic elements of the Gospel message.
- Recognize that believers are to teach the same message Jesus taught.
- Recognize that teaching and preaching should be accompanied with the demonstration of  God's power.
- Identify the Bible as the basis for instruction on the Kingdom of God.

**KEY VERSES:**

**And as ye go, preach, saying, The Kingdom of Heaven is at hand.**

**Heal the sick, cleanse the lepers, raise the dead, cast out  devils:  freely  ye have  received,  freely  give.  (Matthew 10:7-8)**

## INTRODUCTION

In the last chapter you learned of the teaching mission of Jesus which is now the responsibility of believers.  You studied qualities of His lifestyle which should be evident in your life as a teacher.  You learned why, when, where and who Jesus taught.

In this and the following chapter you will learn <u>what</u> Jesus taught.  Jesus did not have a lifetime to train His disciples.  He only had a few short years, so He focused His teaching on important concepts. The content of His message should be the focus of your own teaching mission.

## THE BASIC MESSAGE

The basic message of Jesus can be summarized in one sentence:  <u>He taught all things concerning the Kingdom of God.</u>

All men live in a natural kingdom of this world.  They live in a city or village which is part of a nation. That nation is a kingdom of the world. In addition to the natural kingdoms of this world there are two spiritual kingdoms. Every person is a resident of one of these two kingdoms: The Kingdom of Satan or the Kingdom of God. Unbelievers are part of the Kingdom of Satan. Satan rules their lives. They have an ungodly, immoral, fleshly, sinful lifestyle. Those who have repented from sin and accepted Jesus as their personal Savior are part of God's Kingdom. God is their King and He rules their lives.

The Gospel of the Kingdom of God was the central purpose of Christ's life. He began His earthly ministry by declaring the arrival of the Kingdom:

> **From that time Jesus began to preach, and to say, Repent: For the Kingdom of Heaven is at hand. (Matthew 4:17)**

He ended His earthly ministry by speaking of "things pertaining to the Kingdom":

> **To whom also He shewed Himself alive after His passion by many infallible proofs, being seen of them forty days, and speaking of the things pertaining to the Kingdom of God. (Acts 1:3)**

Between the beginning and ending of His earthly ministry, the Kingdom of God was the focus of His teaching. He said:

> **I must preach the Kingdom of God to other cities also; for therefore am I sent. (Luke 4:43)**

The parables of Jesus focused on the Kingdom. His miracles were a demonstration of the Kingdom of God in action. Jesus taught people how to enter the Kingdom through the born-again experience (John 3). This is evangelism. Jesus also taught people how to live as part of God's Kingdom by developing a Kingdom lifestyle. (For an example, read Matthew 5-7). This is discipleship.

Because of the importance of the subject of God's Kingdom, Harvestime International Institute offers a course entitled *"Kingdom Living."* If you have not already studied this course it is important that you do so. It contains detailed teaching on the Gospel of the Kingdom.

Another course offered by Harvestime International Institute, *"Foundations Of Faith,"* provides teaching on the basic truths [spiritual "foundations"] on which the Kingdom rests.

If you are taking the Institute courses in their suggested order, you have already studied these courses and understand how to enter and live as part of God's Kingdom. It is this message you must preach and teach to others.

# BASIC ELEMENTS OF THE GOSPEL

There is a passage in the New Testament that summarizes the basic Gospel message:

> **Moreover, brethren, I declare unto you the Gospel which I preached unto you, which also ye have received, and where in ye stand:**
>
> **By which also we are saved, if ye keep in memory what I preached unto you, unless you have believed in vain.**
>
> **For I delivered unto you first of all that which I also received, how that Christ died for our sins according to the Scriptures;**
>
> **And that He was buried, and that He rose again the third day according to the Scriptures.   (I Corinthians 15:1-4)**

The basic elements of the Gospel message are that Jesus died for our sins according to the Scriptures, He was buried, and He rose again according to the Scriptures.  When you preach or teach the Gospel of the Kingdom your message should include these basic facts.  Jesus is the focus of the Gospel message.  Biblical teaching should always concern either evangelism [how to enter the Kingdom of God] or discipleship [how to live in the Kingdom of God].

# THE WORD OF GOD

Jesus taught God's message of truth:

> **...Master, we know that thou art true, and teachest the way of God in truth...  (Matthew 22:16)**

He taught doctrine:

> **And He taught the many things by parables and said unto them in His doctrine...  (Mark 4:2)**

You will learn as you study the teaching methods of Jesus that He used Old Testament Scriptures frequently.  Biblical teaching should include the total revelation of God's Word, as it is the basis of instruction which teaches us how to live in the Kingdom of God:

> **All Scripture is given by inspiration of God and is profitable for doctrine, for reproof, for correction, for instruction in righteousness:**
>
> **That the man of God may be perfect, thoroughly furnished unto all good works.  (II Timothy 3:16-17)**

# THE COMMISSION TO BELIEVERS

Believers are commissioned by Jesus to teach and preach the same message: The Gospel of the Kingdom of God.  Jesus told His followers:

**And as ye go, preach, saying, The Kingdom of Heaven is at hand.**

**Heal the sick, cleanse the lepers, raise the dead, cast out devils:  freely ye have  received, freely  give.  (Matthew 10:7-8)**

**And He said unto them, Go ye into all the world and preach the Gospel to every creature.  (Mark 16:15)**

The teaching of Jesus always included emphasis on reproduction.  Those who became part of God's Kingdom had a responsibility to reproduce and bring others into the Kingdom.  This is how the Kingdom would continue to grow and spread throughout the world.  New converts in the Kingdom must become disciples.  A disciple is a pupil of a teacher who learns and puts into practice what he learns.  Disciples must then become apostles.  An apostle is one sent forth with a special commission representing the sender.

Because you received the Gospel freely from Jesus, you are to share it freely with others.  The pattern is summarized by the Apostle Paul:

**And the things that thou hast heard of me among many witnesses, the same commit thou to faithful men, who shall be able to teach others also. (II Timothy 2:2)**

It is important that you are faithful to the commission of spreading the Gospel of the Kingdom because when you have completed the task, the kingdoms of this world will end:

**And this Gospel of the Kingdom shall be preached in all the world for a witness unto all nations; and then shall the end come.  (Matthew 24:14)**

## THE DEMONSTRATION OF POWER

The message of the Kingdom of God is not just to be a verbal message.  It is to be accompanied by a demonstration of the power of the Kingdom in action.  Jesus said:

**The Spirit of the Lord is upon me, because He hath anointed me  to  preach the  Gospel  to  the poor, He hath sent me to heal the brokenhearted, to preach deliverance to the captives, and recovering of sight to the blind, to set at liberty them that are bruised.  (Luke 4:18)**

The Kingdom of God was demonstrated as Jesus taught:

> **And Jesus went about all Galilee, teaching in their synagogues, and preaching the Gospel of the Kingdom, and healing all manner of sickness and all manner of disease among the people. (Matthew 4:23)**

> **Whosoever therefore shall break one of these least commandments, and shall teach men so, he shall be called the least in the Kingdom of heaven: but whosoever shall do and teach them, the same shall be called great in the Kingdom of Heaven. (Matthew 5:19)**

When Jesus commissioned His followers to spread the Gospel of the Kingdom, He told them to...

> **Heal the sick, cleanse the lepers, raise the dead, cast out devils: freely ye have received, freely give. (Matthew 10:8)**

The message of the Kingdom of God must be accompanied by a demonstration of His power that changes lives. Because of the importance of this subject, Harvestime International Institute offers a course entitled *"Power Principles."* The teaching tactics you learn in this course must be combined with the demonstration of power, so it is important that you study and apply the principles taught in both courses.

# SELF-TEST

1. Write the Key Verses from memory.

_____

_____

_____

_____

2. What was the basic message taught by Jesus Christ?

_____

_____

3. Give a Biblical reference which summarizes the basic elements of the Gospel message.

_____

4. Is this statement true or false:  Believers are to teach and preach the same message Jesus did.

The statement is_____.

5. The teaching and preaching of the Gospel is to be accompanied by the demonstration of

God's _____.

6. What is the basic book for instruction which teaches about the Kingdom of God?

_____

(Answers to self-tests are provided at the conclusion of the final chapter in this manual.)

# FOR FURTHER STUDY

1. Obtain the Harvestime International Institute course entitled *"Kingdom Living"* for further study of the spiritual Kingdom of which Jesus taught.

2. *"Foundations Of Faith"* is a Harvestime International Institute course which explains basic truths upon which the Gospel of the Kingdom of God rests. It is important that you learn these also.

3. Obtain the Harvestime International Institute course, *"Power Principles,"* for further study of how the demonstration of power is to be combined with teaching and preaching.

# CHAPTER FOUR

## A TEACHER COME FROM GOD: THE MESSAGE - PART II

**OBJECTIVES:**

Upon completion of this chapter you will be able to:

- Continue studying the message taught by Jesus.
- Use this lesson to share the teachings of Jesus Christ with others.

**KEY VERSE:**

**This then is the message which we have heard of Him, and declare unto you, that God is light, and in Him is no darkness at all. (I John 1:5)**

### INTRODUCTION

The general message of Jesus was the Gospel of the Kingdom. But what were the specific details of His teaching?

### HOW TO STUDY WHAT JESUS TAUGHT

1. Obtain a red letter edition of the Bible. This is a Bible which has everything Jesus said printed in red. You can study His teachings in detail by studying all that is printed in red in the books of Matthew, Mark, Luke, John and Acts chapter One. (If you cannot obtain such a Bible, then use a regular Bible and underline everything Jesus said.)

2. Study Acts and the Epistles [Romans through Jude] in the New Testament. Observe what these believers taught as they fulfilled the teaching commission given by Jesus.

3. Use the following outline to study and teach what Jesus taught.

### TEACHING WHAT JESUS TAUGHT

This outline lists references for all the subjects Jesus taught on during His earthly ministry. The teachings are grouped according to general subject matter.

There are four main books in the Bible which record the teachings of Jesus. These are the books of Matthew, Mark, Luke, and John. Often a certain teaching of Jesus is repeated in all four books. The references in this chapter are organized to combine these similar accounts. This outline will help you teach important truths Jesus taught. It will equip you to share the message of His Gospel with the nations of the world.

Note: Because of the reference format of this chapter, there is no "Self-Test" or "For Further Study" section.

## THE GODHEAD

### GOD THE FATHER:

Matthew 11:27; 19:17,26; 22:32; 23:9
Mark 12:26-27,29; 10:18,27
Luke 10:22; 18:19,27; 20:37-38
John 4:24; 5:17,37; 6:46; 10:29; 14:28,31; 15:8

### THE SON, JESUS CHRIST:

#### Divine Nature:

Matthew 9:5-6; 10:32-33; 11:4-6,27; 12:6,41-42; 16:13,15,17,27; 21:42; 22:42-45; 23:10; 26:53,64; 27:11; 28:18

Mark 2:9-11,28; 8:27,29; 12:10-11,35-37; 14:62; 15:2

Luke 5:23-24; 6:5; 7:22-23; 9:18,20; 10:22; 11:20,31-32; 19:40; 20:17-18,41-44; 22:69-70; 23:3

John 1:51; 3:13; 4:10,26,32; 5:17,19-23,26-27,30-32,34,36-37,39,41; 6:27,29,35,46,51,62; 7:17-18; 8:14,16-19,23,25,29,42, 50,54-56,58; 9:35,37; 10:25,30,34-38; 12:30,44-45; 13:31-32; 14:1,6,7,9-11,20; 15:23; 16:15,27-28; 17:1-3,5,8,10-11,21-24,28-29; 18:36-37; 19:11

#### Human Nature:

Matthew 3:15; 8:20; 11:19; 26:10-13,38-39,42,45; 27:46
Mark 14:7-9,26,34,36,41; 15:34
Luke 7:34; 9:58; 22:28,42; 24:39,41
John 4:7; 12:7-8; 19:26,28; 20:27; 21:5,12

## His Mission:

Matthew 4:4; 5:17; 9:12-13; 10:34-36; 11:15; 15:26; 18:11-13; 21:33-40

Mark 1:38; 2:17; 4:21-22; 7:16,27; 12:1-9

Luke 2:49; 4:18-19,21,23-27,43; 5:31-32; 8:16,17; 11:30,33; 12:2-3,14,49,51-53; 13:32-33; 19:10; 20:9-16

John 3:19-21; 4:13,14,34; 5:25,28-30; 6:38-40,50,55,56,58; 7:7,16; 8:12,26; 9:3-5,39; 10:1-5,7,9-18,27-29; 11:4,9,10; 12:26,27,47-50; 13:20; 18:15,16,37

## His Ministry:

Matthew 9:15,37,38; 12:25-30; 20:28
Mark 2:19; 3:23-27; 10:45
Luke 5:34; 11:17-23
John 2:4; 3:11; 4:35-38; 12:35,36

## His Position:

Matthew 10:29-30; 11:28-31

Luke 4:18,19; 8:52

John 6:37; 7:37; 10:9; 11:25,26; 12:32; 14:1,2,6,13,14,16,27; 15:1,2,4-6,9-11,15-16,18,19; 16:1,4,23,24,33

## THE HOLY SPIRIT:

Matthew 10:19,20; 12:31,32; 28:19
Mark 3:28,29
Luke 12:10-12
John 3:8; 6:63; 16:7-11,13,14; 20:22
Acts 1:8

## THE KINGDOM OF GOD AND HEAVEN

Matthew 4:17; 5:20; 6:33; 7:21; 8:11; 10:7; 11:11-13; 13:3-8,11,18-33; 37-50,52; 16:28; 22:2-14; 25:14-30; 26:29

Mark 4:3-8,11-20,26-29; 9:1; 14:25

Luke 8:5-15; 9:27; 10:11; 11:20; 12:31; 13:18-21,29,30; 17:20,21; 19:12-27; 21:31; 22:18

## THE CHURCH

Matthew 5:13-15; 12:48-50; 16:18,19; 18:17-20; 21:13; 23:16-21; 24:22,31
Mark 3:33-35; 11:17; 12:10; 13:20,27
Luke 8:21; 11:23; 12:32; 19:26
John 2:16; 4:23,24; 13:35; 17:20,21; 20:23

## THE LAW, THE SCRIPTURES, THE PROPHETS

Matthew 5:17,18; 7:12; 8:4; 11:13; 21:42; 26:54
Mark 1:44; 12:10,11; 14:21,29
Luke 5:14; 10:26,28; 16:16,17,29-31; 17:14; 18:31; 21:22; 22:22,37; 24:25,26,44,46
John 5:39,45-47; 7:12,19; 8:17,18; 10:34-36; 15:25

## THE WORD

Matthew 4:4; 7:24-27; 10:27; 11:15; 13:3-9,19-23; 28:19,20

Mark 4:3-9,14-20,23,24; 13:31

Luke 4:4,18,19,43; 6:46-49; 8:5-8,10-15,18; 10:24

John 3:11; 5:24,25,28,46,47; 6:63; 7:17,18; 8:14,31,32,38,45-57; 10:27; 12:47-50; 14:10,21,23-25; 15:7,10,12,14,15,17,20,22; 16:12,13,25,33; 17:6-8,13,14,19,20,25,26; 18:20,37

## THE OLD AND NEW DISPENSATIONS

The "old dispensation" refers to the way God dealt with mankind during the period recorded in the Old Testament. It includes government by law and the various sacrifices for sin described in the book of Leviticus.

The "new dispensation" refers to the new way God dealt with mankind from the time of the earthly ministry of Jesus Christ. It is known as the period of grace during which the sacrifice for sin was made once and for all through the death of Jesus on the cross.

### THE PROPHET ANNOUNCING THE NEW DISPENSATION:

A man named John the Baptist was the prophet sent from God to announce to men the new dispensation. Jesus taught concerning him in the following passages:

39

Matthew 7:11; 11:7-11,14,18; 21:25
Mark 9:13; 11:30
Luke 7:24-28,33; 20:4
John 5:33,35

## TEACHINGS ON THE DISPENSATIONS:

The teachings of Jesus regarding the old and new dispensations are found in the following passages:

Matthew 5:17; 11:27; 26:27,28
Mark 14:24
Luke 10:22; 16:16; 22:20
John 4:23; 5:25; 6:32,33,49,58
I Corinthians 11:25

# THE DISCIPLES

Jesus chose twelve men to be His disciples during His earthly ministry.

## GENERAL TEACHINGS:

The following teachings were given to the disciples as a group:

Matthew 13:11,16,17,51; 16:8-11; 17:7; 18:18; 21:2,3; 23:10; 24:9; 26:38,40,45
Mark 4:11,12,35; 6:31; 8:17-20; 11:2,3; 13:9,11,13; 14:27,32, 34,41; 16:15
Luke 8:10,22; 10:23-24; 19:30,31; 21:14-19; 22:28-30,35,36,38; 24:49
John 6:61,67,70; 12:30; 14:25,31; 15:12,16-20,27; 16:2,3,27,32; 20:21-23

## SPECIFIC TEACHINGS:

The following teachings were directed to specific disciples:

## Peter and Andrew:

Matthew 4:19
Mark 1:17

## Matthew:

Matthew 9:9
Mark 2:14

**Peter:**

Matthew 16:17-19,23; 17:25-27; 26:34
Mark 8:33; 14:30,37
Luke 5:4,10; 22:31,32,34,51
John 1:42; 13:7,8,10,36,38; 18:11; 21:15-19,22

**Thomas:**

John 20:27,29

**Philip:**

John 14:9

**Judas Iscariot:**

John 13:27


## SENDING OF THE DISCIPLES

Special words were spoken by Jesus when He sent His disciples out to share the Gospel of the Kingdom.

### WORDS SPOKEN TO THE TWELVE DISCIPLES:

Matthew 10:5-42
Mark 6:10,11
Luke 9:3-5

### WORDS SPOKEN TO THE SEVENTY:

Luke 10:3-12,16,19,20

## THE PRAYERS OF JESUS

These references concern the recorded prayers of Jesus. In addition to learning what Jesus taught about prayer, it is important to examine how He put His teachings into practice in His own prayer life.

Matthew 6:9-13; 11:25,26; 26:36,39,42

Mark 14:36
Luke 10:21; 11:2-4; 22:42
John 11:41,42; 17:1-26

## EVENTS IN THE LIFE OF JESUS

Jesus taught concerning special events that were to happen in His own life and used special occasions to share God's truths. These include the following:

## SUFFERING AND TEMPTATION:

Matthew 17:12; 13:57; 26:38
Mark 6:4; 9:12; 14:34
Luke 4:24; 9:22; 17:25; 22:28; 24:46

## THE LAST SUPPER:

Matthew 26:18,26-29
Mark 14:13-15,22,24,25
Luke 22:8,10-12,15-20
I Corinthians 11:24,25

## THE BETRAYAL:

Matthew 17:22; 26:2,21,23-25,46,50,55
Mark 14:18,20,21,42,48,49
Luke 22:21,22,48,52,53
John 13:18,19,26; 18:4,5,7,8,23

## THE CRUCIFIXION:

Luke 9:44; 22:37
John 3:14; 8:28; 12:31,32

## WORDS ON THE CROSS:

Matthew 27:46
Mark 15:34
Luke 23:34,43,46
John 19:26,27,28,30

## DEATH, RESURRECTION, AND ASCENSION:

Matthew 12:40; 17:19,22,23; 20:18,19; 26:12,31,32

Mark 9:31; 10:33,34; 14:8,27,28

Luke 5:35; 9:22; 12:50; 18:31-33

John 2:19; 3:13; 6:62; 7:33,34; 8:21; 10:17,18; 12:7,23,24; 13:33; 14:19,29; 16:5-7,16,19-22,25,26,32; 20:17

## WORDS SPOKEN AFTER THE RESURRECTION:

Matthew 28:9,10,18-20
Mark 16:15-18
Luke 24:17,19,25,26,36,38,39,41,44,46-49
John 20:15-17,19,21-23,26,27; 21:5,6,10,12,19,22
Acts 1:4,5,7,8

# PROPHECY

Jesus taught much on the subject of prophecy. A prophecy is a revelation of things which have not yet happened. It is a message from God concerning the future. The prophetic subjects Jesus taught on included:

## THE SECOND COMING OF JESUS CHRIST:

Matthew 24:6-47; 25:1-13; 26:64
Mark 2:20; 8:38; 13:7-36; 14:62

## JERUSALEM:

Matthew 5:34,35; 23:37-39; 24:2
Mark 13:2
Luke 13:34,35; 19:42-44; 21:20-24; 23:28-31
John 4:21

## THE JEWS:

Matthew 8:11,12; 10:6; 11:16-19; 15:24,26; 21:31,32; 22:2-7
Mark 7:27
Luke 7:31-35; 21:24; 22:67,68
John 4:22; 7:19,21; 8:37-47,49; 9:41; 10:26,32; 18:20,36

## THE SCRIBES, PHARISEES, AND SADDUCEES:

Matthew 12:34; 15:7-9,14; 16:6; 23:2-7,13-15,25-27,29-36
Mark 7:6; 8:15; 12:38-40
Luke 11:39,40-44,46-52; 12:1; 20:46,47
John 5:42

## THE GENTILES:

Matthew 8:11; 21:43; 22:8-10; 24:14; 28:19
Mark 13:10; 16:15
Luke 13:29; 24:46,47
John 10:16

## FALSE PROPHETS AND FALSE TEACHINGS:

Matthew 7:15-18,20; 24:4,5,11,23,24,26
Mark 13:5,6,21,22
Luke 6:39,43,44; 17:1,2,22,23; 21:8
John 10:1,8

## SIN

A simple definition for sin is that it is the transgression or breaking of God's law. Jesus taught concerning sin:

## SATAN AND SIN:

Matthew 4:10; 12:26,27; 13:19; 16:23; 25:41
Mark 3:23,26; 4:15; 8:33
Luke 4:8; 10:18; 11:18,19; 22:31
John 8:34-36; 14:30

## BLASPHEMY:

Matthew 12:31,32; 15:19
Mark 3:28,29; 7:21,22
Luke 12:10

## SKEPTICISM:

Matthew 14:31; 17:17,20
Mark 2:8; 9:19; 16:16

Luke 9:41

John 3:11,12,18; 4:48; 5:38,40,43-47; 6:64; 8:24,45-47; 12:47,48; 15:22,24,

## HYPOCRISY:

Matthew 6:2,16; 15:7,8; 23:13-15,25,27-29
Mark 7:6; 12:40
Luke 11:44; 12:1; 20:47

## PRIDE:

Matthew 23:5-7,12
Mark 7:21,22; 12:38,39
Luke 11:43; 14:11; 20:46

## ANGER:

Matthew 5:22

## MURDER:

Matthew 5:21; 15:19; 19:17,18
Mark 7:21; 10:19
Luke 18:20
John 8:44

## ADULTERY, FORNICATION, LASCIVIOUSNESS:

Matthew 5:27,28,32; 15:19; 19:9,11,12,17,18
Mark 7:21,22; 10:11,12,19
Luke 16:18; 18:20

## DIVORCE:

Matthew 5:31,32; 19:8,9
Mark 10:3,5,11,12
Luke 16:18

## THEFT:

Matthew 15:19; 19:17,18
Mark 7:21,22; 10:19
Luke 18:20

## FALSE WITNESS, DECEIT, FRAUD:

Matthew 15:19; 19:17,18
Mark 7:21,22; 10:19
Luke 18:20
John 8:44

## EVIL THOUGHTS, EVIL EYE, WICKEDNESS, FOOLISHNESS:

Matthew 6:23; 9:4; 15:19; 20:15
Mark 7:21,22
Luke 11:34

## COVETOUSNESS:

Mark 7:21,22
Luke 12:15-21

## MATERIALISM AND WORLDLINESS:

Matthew 6:19-21,24; 12:39; 13:3,22; 16:4; 24:38,39
Mark 4:3,7,18,19; 8:12
Luke 8:14;  9:60; 10:41,42; 11:29; 14:16-24; 16:1-9,13,15; 17:26-29; 21:34
John 4:48; 6:27

## PROCRASTINATION:

To procrastinate means to continuously delay doing something.

Matthew 24:45-51
Luke 12:42-47; 13:25-28; 14:16-20

## JUDGING:

Matthew 7:1-5; 12:7
Mark 4:24
Luke 6:37,41,42
John 8:7,10,11,15

## BLINDNESS OF HEART:

Matthew 13:13-15; 15:14; 16:2,3
Mark 4:12; 8:18,21
Luke 8:10; 12:54-56

## BACKSLIDING:

To backslide means to turn from following Jesus.

Matthew 12:43-45
Luke 11:24-26

## SACRILEGE:

Sacrilege is the violation of that which is sacred: Matthew 7:6

## DENUNCIATIONS:

Matthew 10:14,15; 11:22,23; 12:34,41,42; 13:13-15; 16:4; 18:7; 21:19; 23:13-15,25,27,29,33-36
Mark 6:11; 8:12; 11:14
Luke 6:24-26; 9:5; 10:10-15; 11:29,32,42,44,46,47,49-52

## RIGHTEOUSNESS

Jesus spent much of His earthly ministry teaching on the subject of righteousness, how one should live in right relation to God, others, and self.

## THE CALLS TO RIGHTEOUSNESS:

Matthew 4:19; 8:22; 9:9; 14:29
Mark 1:17; 2:14; 4:24; 10:21; 19:21
Luke 5:27; 9:59,60; 18:22
John 1:38,39,43; 12:26; 21:19

## FAITH:

Matthew 8:10,13,26; 9:22,28,29; 14:27; 15:18; 17:20; 21:22
Mark 4:40; 5:34,36; 6:50; 7:29; 9:23; 10:52; 11:22-24; 16:16-18
Luke 7:9,50; 8:25,48,50; 17:6,19; 18:8,42
John 3:18; 6:20,29; 7:38; 9:35; 11:15,25,26,40,42; 14:1,12; 16:31; 20:27,29

**SALVATION THROUGH FAITH:**

Mark 16:16
John 3:14-16,18; 5:24; 6:40,47; 11:25,26

**REPENTANCE:**

Matthew 4:17; 21:28-32
Mark 1:15
Luke 13:2-5; 15:4-32

**BAPTISM:**

Matthew 21:25; 28:19
Mark 11:30; 16:16
Luke 20:4
John 3:5
Acts 1:5

**REGENERATION:**

Matthew 9:16,17
Mark 2:21,22
Luke 5:36-39
John 3:3,5-8,10

**WORKS:**

Matthew 5:16; 7:16-27; 12:33; 13:3,4,8,23; 21:19
Mark 3:33-35; 4:3,4,8,20; 11:14
Luke 6:43,44,46-49; 10:30-37; 13:6-9
John 7:17; 10:37,38; 15:8,16

**THE GREAT COMMANDMENTS:**

Matthew 7:12; 22:37-40
Mark 12:29-31
Luke 6:31

**LOVE:**

Matthew 5:43-47; 7:12
Luke 6:27,28,32-35

John 13:34,35; 14:23,24; 15:12,13,17

## CHARITY:

Matthew 5:42; 6:1-4; 19:21
Mark 10:21; 12:43,44
Luke 6:30,38; 11:41; 12:33,34; 14:12-14; 16:9; 18:22; 21:3,4

## FORGIVENESS AND RECONCILIATION:

Matthew 5:23-26; 6:14,15; 9:2,5,6; 16:18,19; 18:18,22-35
Mark 2:5,9-11; 11:25,26
Luke 5:20,23,24; 6:37; 7:40-48; 12:58,59; 17:3,4; 23:34; 24:46,47
John 20:23

## MERCY:

Matthew 5:7; 9:13; 18:15-17,27,33
Luke 6:36

## SELF-RENUNCIATION:

Matthew 10:37-39; 16:24-26
Mark 8:34-37
Luke 9:23-25; 14:26,27-33; 17:33
John 12:25

## PURITY AND SINGLENESS OF HEART:

Matthew 5:8,27,28; 6:22-24; 9:4; 12:34,35; 15:10,11,16-20
Mark 7:18-23; 10:15
Luke 4:12; 6:45; 11:34-36,41; 16:13; 18:17

## PURITY AND SPEECH:

Matthew 5:33-37; 12:36,37; 23:20-22

## OVERCOMING THE FLESH:

Matthew 5:29,30; 6:16-18; 17:21; 18:8,9
Mark 9:29,43-49

## OBEDIENCE AND SUBMISSION:

Matthew 26:39,42; 28:19,20
Mark 14:36
Luke 22:42
John 7:17,18; 8:29,50; 14:15,21; 15:14; 18:11

## SUBMISSION TO AUTHORITY:

Matthew 17:25-27; 22:19-21
Mark 12:15-17
Luke 20:24,25

## FAITHFULNESS AND WATCHFULNESS:

Matthew 24:42-47; 25:13; 26:41
Mark 13:33-37; 14:38
Luke 12:35-40,42-44,47,48; 16:10-12; 21:36; 22:40,46

## STEADFASTNESS AND PERSEVERANCE:

Matthew 5:13; 10:22; 13:3-9,18-23; 24:13
Mark 4:3-9,13-20; 9:50; 13:13
Luke 9:62; 14:34,35
John 8:31,32

## PATIENCE:

Luke 21:19
Acts 1:7

## COURAGE:

Matthew 8:26; 14:27; 17:7
Mark 4:40; 5:36; 6:50
Luke 8:50
John 6:20

## NON-RESISTANCE:

Matthew 5:38-41,43-45; 26:52
Luke 6:27-30

## HUMILITY AND SIMPLICITY:

Matthew 5:3,5; 11:25,26; 18:3,4; 20:25-27; 23:8,11,12
Mark 9:33,35; 10:15,42-44
Luke 9:48; 14:8-11; 18:14,17; 22:25-27
John 13:7,8,10,12-17

## TRUST IN GOD'S PROVISION:

Matthew 6:25-34
Luke 12:6,7,22,24-32

## GRATITUDE:

Matthew 8:4
Mark 1:44; 5:19
Luke 5:14; 7:40-48,50; 8:39; 17:17,18

## TOLERATION:

Mark 9:39-41
Luke 9:50

## DUTY:

Luke 17:7-10

## PERFECTION:

Matthew 5:48; 7:13,14; 19:21
Mark 10:21
Luke 6:40; 12:57; 13:24; 18:22

## THE BEATITUDES:

Matthew 5:3-12; 11:6; 13:16
Luke 6:20-23; 7:23; 10:23; 11:28

## SPECIAL TEACHINGS

Jesus taught on other important subjects which we have grouped together under this heading of "Special Teachings." These include:

## ATONEMENT FOR SIN:

Matthew 17:12; 20:18,19,28; 26:24,31,39,42

Mark 9:12; 10:33,34,45; 14:21,24,36

Luke 9:22,56; 13:34,35; 18:31-33; 19:10; 21:28; 22:19,22,37,42;  24:26,44,46,47

John 3:13-16,18; 5:39; 6:38-40,51; 8:24,28,56; 10:7,9-11,15-18,36; 11:25,26; 12:24,27,32,47; 13:7,8; 14:19; 15:13; 16:7,20,22,33; 17:1-4,19-21,23; 18:11; 19:30

I Corinthians 11:24,25

## EQUALITY UNDER THE ATONEMENT:

Matthew 20:1-15

## PRAYER:

Matthew 6:5-13; 7:7-11; 18:19,20; 21:22; 26:41
Mark 11:24; 14:38
Luke 11:2-13; 18:2-8,10-14; 22:40,46
John 4:24; 14:13,14; 15:7; 16:23,24;

## THE LETTER AND THE SPIRIT:

Matthew 15:3-8,10,11,16-20; 23:16-26,28
Mark 7:6-8,14,15,18-23
Luke 11:39,40,42,44
John 6:63; 7:24

## FOREORDINATION:

Matthew 15:13; 20:23; 22:14; 24:22,31
Mark 10:40; 13:20,27
Luke 18:7
John 6:37,43-45,64,65; 15:16

## PROFESSION OF FAITH:

Matthew 10:32,33
Mark 5:19; 8:38
Luke 8:39; 9:26; 12:8,9

## PERSONAL ACCOUNTABILITY:

Matthew 13:12; 22:11-13
Mark 4:23-25
Luke 8:18; 12:47,48
John 9:41

## LABOR AND SELF-DEVELOPMENT:

Matthew 20:6; 25:14-30
Luke 19:12-26

## THE SABBATH:

Matthew 12:3-5,8,11,12
Mark 2:25-28; 3:4
Luke 6:3-5,9; 13:15,16; 14:3,5

## MARRIAGE:

Matthew 19:4-6; 22:30
Mark 10:6-9; 12:25
Luke 20:34,35

## CHILDREN:

Matthew 18:3-6,10,14; 19:14; 21:16
Mark 9:37,42; 10:14,15
Luke 9:48; 18:16,17

## THE POOR:

Matthew 11:5; 19:21; 26:11
Mark 10:21; 14:7
Luke 4:18,21; 6:20; 14:13,14; 18:22
John 12:8

## THE RICH:

Matthew 19:23,24
Mark 10:23-25
Luke 14:12; 16:19-31; 18:24,25

## SORROW:

Matthew 5:4; 10:38; 11:28; 16:24; 23:38,39; 24:7,8; 26:38,39,42
Mark 4:16,17; 8:34; 13:19; 14:34,36
Luke 6:21; 9:23; 14:27; 21:22-26; 22:42; 23:28-30; 24:38
John 12:27; 14:1,27; 16:5,6,20-22; 18:11

## PEACE AND REST:

Matthew 9:22; 10:13; 11:28-30; 26:45
Mark 4:39; 5:34; 6:31; 9:50; 14:41
Luke 7:50; 8:48; 10:5,6,41,42; 12:29; 19:42; 24:36
John 14:1,23,27; 16:33; 20:19,21,26

## JOY:

Matthew 5:11; 6:17; 9:2; 13:44; 14:27; 18:12,13; 25:21,23
Mark 6:50
Luke 6:21-23; 10:20; 11:36; 15:4-10,32
John 4:36; 8:56; 13:17; 15:11; 16:20-22,24; 17:13

## WISDOM:

Matthew 7:24; 10:16; 11:15,25; 13:51; 15:16; 16:2,3; 21:16; 24:45-47
Mark 4:12; 7:14,16; 8:17,18,21
Luke 6:47,48; 8:10; 10:21; 12:42-44,54-56; 16:1-8
John 8:12; 9:41; 12:46

## DEATH AND PARADISE:

Matthew 8:22; 9:24; 10:8,28; 16:28; 17:9,23; 22:32
Mark 5:39; 9:1,31; 10:34; 12:25-27; 14:34
Luke 7:22; 9:27,60; 12:4,5,20; 16:31; 18:33; 20:35-38; 23:43; 24:46
John 5:21,25,28,29; 6:39,40,49,58; 10:17,18; 11:4,14; 12:24; 15:13

## SPECIAL WORDS TO INDIVIDUALS

This final group of teachings of Jesus are special words spoken to individuals during His earthly ministry. They include the following:

## NATHANAEL:

John 1:47,48,50

**THE WOMAN OF SAMARIA:**

John 4:7,16-18

**ZACCHAEUS, THE PUBLICAN:**

Luke 19:5,9

**THE BLIND MEN OF JERICHO:**

Matthew 20:32

**THE QUESTIONING SCRIBES:**

Mark 9:16

**THE SONS OF ZEBEDEE:**

Matthew 20:21-23
Mark 10:36,38-40

**JESUS' BRETHREN:**

John 7:6-8

**THE QUESTIONING SCRIBE:**

Mark 12:34

**MARTHA:**

Luke 10:41,42

**THE CHIEF PRIESTS AND THE ELDERS:**

Matthew 21:24,25,27
Mark 11:29,30,33
Luke 20:3,4,8

## THE DISCIPLES OF THE PHARISEES WITH THE HERODIANS:

Matthew 22:18
Luke 20:23

## THE HIGH PRIEST:

John 18:21

## PILATE:

John 18:34

# CHAPTER FIVE

## A TEACHER SENT FROM GOD:  THE METHODS - PART I

**OBJECTIVES:**

Upon completion of this chapter you will be able to explain how Jesus used the following teaching methods:

- Miracles
- Authority
- Love And Compassion
- Association And Imitation
- Response
- Delegation
- Environment
- Visual Demonstration
- The Principle Of Gradual Learning
- Grouping Of Students

**KEY VERSE:**

> **And Jesus went about all the cities and villages, teaching in their synagogues, and preaching the gospel of the kingdom, and healing every sickness and every disease among the people.  (Matthew 9:35)**

## INTRODUCTION

You have learned when, where, why, and what Jesus taught during His earthly ministry.  In this and the following chapter you will study _how_ Jesus taught.  These lessons focus on the methods He used in teaching.  A method is a plan, system, procedure, or way of doing something. The teaching methods of Jesus refer to _how_ He taught.

Often, the Church has been content to use secular educational methods rather than those revealed in God's Word. The best methods for Biblical teaching are those which Jesus used and proved to be effective.  This lesson focuses on general methods which accompanied the teaching of Jesus. The  following chapter concerns specific methods of verbal instruction.

# MIRACLES

You have learned that a teacher's message should be accompanied by the demonstration of God's power. This demonstration of power attracts people to hear the Word of God:

> **And when the sabbath day was come, He began to teaching the synagogue: and many hearing Him were astonished saying, From whence hath this man these things? And what wisdom is this which is given unto Him, that even such mighty works are wrought by his hands? (Mark 6:2) (See also Matthew 13:54).**

Jesus used miracles to prepare the hearts of people to receive messages. Read the story of Jesus healing the man blind from birth in John 9. As a result of his healing the witness of God's power went to his neighbors (9:8), the religious leaders (9:13), and his family (9:18). In John 9:41-50, Jesus used the healing to teach a message from God to the religious leaders.

The miracles of Jesus ministered to people at their point of need. As you study more about miracles in the "For Further Study" section of this lesson you will see how His miracles met material, physical, emotional, spiritual, mental, and natural needs. Demons were cast out, the dead were raised, the sick were healed, the hungry fed, and those in need of deliverance received it.

There is no greater method to illustrate and confirm a Biblical message than the demonstration of God's power. This power meets human need and brings change to lives. This is why Jesus delegated spiritual power to His followers:

> **And He called unto Him the twelve, and began to send them forth by two and two; and gave them power over unclean spirits. (Mark 6:7)**
>
> **And as ye go, preach, saying, The Kingdom of Heaven is at hand.**
>
> **Heal the sick, cleanse the lepers, raise the dead, cast out devils; freely ye have received freely give. (Matthew 10:7-8)**
>
> **Verily, verily, I say unto you, He that believeth on me, the works that I do shall he do also; and greater works than these shall he do, because I go unto my Father. (John 14:12)**

# AUTHORITY

Jesus taught with authority. "Authority" means to exercise power of command. Like miracles, teaching with authority attracted listeners:

**And they were astonished at His doctrine: for He taught them as one that had authority, and not as the scribes. (Mark 1:22) (See also Matthew 21:23).**

Some modern educators encourage the teacher to become "one of the group" rather than teach with authority. But Jesus taught with authority. The authority of Jesus was given by God. Before returning to Heaven, Jesus gave us spiritual authority:

**As my Father hath sent me [with power and authority] so send I you. (John 20:21)**

Jesus promised authority [power] to believers to enable them to teach and preach as witnesses of the Gospel:

**But ye shall receive power after that the Holy Ghost is come upon you; and ye shall be witnesses unto me both in Jerusalem, and in all Judaea, and in Samaria and unto the uttermost part of the earth. (Acts 1:8)**

Education, social position, or natural ability is not the basis of Biblical authority. Our authority in teaching comes from Jesus Christ.

## LOVE AND COMPASSION

Jesus did not condemn those He taught. Instead, He showed them love and compassion. When the woman was caught in the act of adultery, He did not condemn her (John 8:11). When Mary used expensive perfume to anoint Him, Jesus did not condemn her for wasting what could have been sold to help the poor. He understood the reason behind the act and treated her with love (Matthew 26:10-13).

Jesus had compassion on the blind (Mark 10:46-62) and children (Mark 10:13-16) when His own disciples did not care. Jesus loved even the rich young man who chose riches instead of following Him (Mark 10:17-22). Jesus healed the ear of the soldier who came to arrest Him (Luke 22:50-51). The compassion of Jesus led Him to intercession for the people to whom He ministered (Mark 6:34) and their cities (Luke 19:41).

I Corinthians 13 reveals that any ministry [teaching included] is not effective unless done in love. Teachers must show love, concern, and compassion to students or "it profiteth nothing."

## ASSOCIATION AND IMITATION

When Jesus called His disciples, He had a specific purpose:

**And He ordained twelve, that they should be with Him, and that He might**

**send them forth to preach,**

**And to have power to heal sicknesses, and to cast out devils.**
**(Mark 3:14-15)**

The disciples were first called to be _with_ Jesus, to learn from Him by the example He set. Knowledge was gained by association before it was understood by explanation. The disciples were to be "with" Jesus in an active role. They were not to be just passive listeners. They were to observe and participate in His ministry. Jesus lived and demonstrated what He taught. His example of living His messages is one of the most effective teaching methods you can follow.

Jesus showed His students how to apply Biblical teaching to everyday life. To teach the lesson on prayer, He prayed. To teach the importance of Scripture He quoted from it. To teach the importance of spreading the Gospel, He spread it. To explain God's power, He demonstrated it.

The upright lifestyle of a teacher adds the highest credibility to his message. The teacher must have contact with students in everyday life and ministry situations to provide opportunity for learning by association.

## RESPONSE

From the time He first told His disciples "Follow Me," Jesus continually called for responses to the messages He taught. He told men and women to come to Him and to take up their cross (Mark 8:34-35). He sent them to testify before their families (Mark 5:19) and religious leaders (Luke 5:14). He told some to sell their riches (Mark 10:21), go wash in pools of water (John 9:7) and other similar commands.

Teaching is not complete without the living out of the lessons. You must teach students to act upon what they have been taught. They must become doers of the Word, not just professional listeners:

**But be ye doers of the Word, and not hearers only, deceiving your own selves.**

**For if any be a hearer of the Word, and not a doer, He is like unto a man beholding his natural face in a glass;**

**For he beholdeth himself and goeth his way, and straightway forgetteth what manner of man he was.**

**But whoso looketh into the perfect law of liberty, and continueth therein, he**

being not a forgetful hearer, but a doer of the work, this man shall be blessed in his deed.  (James 1:22-25)

Spiritual growth is not measured by what a student  hears, but by what he does about what he hears.  You must teach so students experience the Word, not just learn information about it. They must come to really know God, not just know about Him.  Learning involves "doing" as well as "teaching."  Jesus demonstrated this in His own ministry:

The former treatise have I made, O Theophilus, of all that Jesus began both to do and teach.  (Acts 1:1)

Jesus said:

Whosoever therefore shall break one of these least commandments, and shall teach men so, he shall be called the least in the Kingdom of Heaven; but whosoever shall do and teach them, the same shall be called great in the Kingdom of Heaven.  (Matthew 5:19)

He taught His disciples to "do" as well as "teach":

And the apostles gathered themselves together unto Jesus, and told Him all things, both what they had done, and what they had taught.  (Mark 6:30)

An opportunity for response from the students should always be provided when you teach.  You will learn more about this in Chapter Ten, "Lesson Planning."  But a call for response must not be cheap emotional appeal.  Jesus made it clear that to respond to the claims of the Gospel would be costly:

And when He had called the people unto Him with His disciples also, He said unto them, Whosoever will come after me, let Him deny Himself and take up His cross, and follow me.

For whosoever will save His life shall lose it; but whosoever shall lose his life for My sake and the Gospel's, the same shall save it.  (Mark 8:34-35)

## DELEGATION

From the beginning of time, God delegated responsibility to people.  He gave them assignments such as naming the animals, and building arks, tabernacles, temples, and walls. Jesus also  delegated spiritual projects to His disciples.  He told them to feed the multitudes (Matthew 14:16).  He sent them out to preach the Gospel and heal the sick (Matthew 10:9-10). He expected them to reproduce spiritually (John 15).

Jesus prepared students to take His place when He returned to Heaven. Gradually, He delegated to them His responsibility for ministry, teaching, and preaching. You should teach as if you are preparing each student to take your place. To properly prepare them, you must delegate responsibility for the Word with which you have entrusted them.

As a teacher, you must have spiritual goals for your students. You must plan lessons and projects for them which will help them achieve these goals. Delegation of responsibility for ministry is an important part of this process.

## ENVIRONMENT

Jesus used the natural environment in which He found people to teach spiritual lessons. The "environment" includes the physical, social and cultural, and spiritual factors which surround a person. It is the society in which a person lives, works, and ministers.

Jesus made each learning situation part of real life. He taught people right where they lived, worked, or ministered. God continues to teach us in natural life situations through the problems and challenges we face each day. (This is the method of Harvestime International Institute. That is why this course comes to you right where YOU live and work.)

Jesus did not rely on the formal lecture hall, Sabbath day class, or pulpit. As you learned in Chapter Two, He took advantage of every casual encounter to teach. Wherever He was, He taught. Jesus used the circumstances of life to teach lessons. When He happened to pass a funeral procession, He raised a man from the dead (Luke 7:11-15). When Jesus was thirsty, He gave a message on living water (John 3). When He saw a poor woman bringing her offering to the temple, He preached a message on giving (Mark 12:41-44).

People learn best when it is related to their environment. What they learn must be practical and apply to the problems they face. The message must minister to their special needs. When you relate the truths of God's Word to everyday life it is called "application." You "apply" what you learn to real life situations.

Such situations vary from culture to culture and differ depending on the audience. This is why you must know your pupils in order to apply the Word to their lives. You will learn more about this in later lessons entitled "Analyzing The Audience" and "Lesson Planning."

## VISUAL DEMONSTRATION

Jesus used visual aids to illustrate His teaching. A "visual" aid is an object, symbol, or action which illustrates what is being taught. For example, when Jesus wanted to teach the childlike attitude necessary to receive Him and enter the Kingdom...

**...He took a child, and set him in the midst of them: and when He had**

**taken him in His arms, He said unto them,**

**Whosoever shall receive one of such children in my name, receiveth me;
and whosoever shall receive me, receiveth not me, but Him that sent me.
(Mark 9:37)**

When Jesus explained the meaning of His death He used the symbols of bread and wine (Mark 14:22-25). When Jesus wanted to teach a lesson regarding humble service He washed the disciples feet (John 13:1-17). Jesus used visual aids such as flowers (Matthew 5:28) and birds (Matthew 5:26) to illustrate what He wanted to teach.

Chapter Seven in this manual, "Teaching Aids," suggests visual aids you can purchase or make, depending on your culture, finances, and availability of materials. But even if you have no money or access to such aids, you can use objects from your own environment to illustrate your teaching. Jesus had no money for equipment or material to create visual aids. He used simple objects from the environment.

## THE PRINCIPLE OF GRADUAL LEARNING

Jesus realized His students could only learn so much at one time. Because of this, He adjusted His teaching to a level they could properly understand:

**And with many such parables spake He the Word unto them, <u>as they were able to hear it</u>. (Mark 4:33)**

**I have yet many things to say unto you, but ye cannot bear them now.
(John 16:12)**

Each group of students and each individual learns at a different rate. The ability of students to learn is affected by many different things. You will learn more about this in Chapter Eight, "Analyzing The Audience."

## GROUPING OF STUDENTS

Jesus adapted His teaching to various groups of students.

## LARGE CROWDS:

Jesus used the lecture method when He taught large crowds. He did not allow for interruptions or invite a response until the end of the lesson. This is best for large groups. Preaching usually always follows this pattern. See Matthew 5-7 for an example.

## SMALL GROUPS:

Most often in small groups Jesus allowed audience participation.  For examples see Mark 8:10-12; 14-21; 27-30.

## INDIVIDUALS:

Jesus used a conversational method with individuals. He talked with them and asked and answered questions.  The method was much like a normal conversation between two people. For examples see John 3 and 4.

# SELF-TEST

1. Write the Key Verse from memory.

_____

_____

For each of the following, summarize what you learned in this lesson. How did Jesus use...

2. Miracles:

_____

_____

3. Authority:

_____

_____

4. Love and Compassion:

_____

_____

5. Association And Imitation:

_____

_____

6. Response:

_____

_____

7. Delegation:

_____

_____

8. Environment:

_____

_____

9. Visual Demonstration:

_____

_____

10. The Principle Of Gradual Learning:

_____

_____

11. Grouping Of Students:

_____

_____

(Answers to self-tests are provided at the conclusion of the final chapter in this manual.)

# FOR FURTHER STUDY

1. Study further on the miracles of Jesus which ministered to human need:

## MIRACLES OF RAISING THE DEAD

-The only son of a widow, as they were bearing him to the grave: Luke 7:11-16
-The daughter of Jairus, the ruler of the synagogue: Mark 5:22-24, 35-43; Matthew 9:18-26; Luke 8:41,42,49-56
-Lazarus, when he had been dead four days: John 11:32-44
-His own body, the third day from interment: Luke 24:1-7; John 19:42-20:14; Mark 16:9-11

## MIRACLES OF CASTING OUT DEVILS

-The man, of an unclean spirit: Mark 1:23-26; Luke 4:33-37
-The demoniac who was blind and dumb: Matthew 12:22-23; Mark 3:19-30; Luke 11:14-23
-The two men possessed of legion, exceeding fierce: Matthew 8:28-34; compare Luke 8:26-39 and Mark 5:1-20
-The dumb man possessed of a devil: Matthew 9:32-35
-The daughter of the Syrophoenician woman: Mark 7:24-30; Matthew 15:22-28
-The lunatic boy, the disciples having failed: Matthew 17:14-21; compare Mark 9:14-39; Luke 9:37-43
-The devil that was dumb: Mark 9:14-26

## MIRACLES OF HEALING

-Nobleman's son, of a fever: John 4:46-54
-Peter's mother-in-law, of a fever: Mark 1:29-31; Matthew 8:14-17; Luke 4:38-39
-A man full of leprosy: Mark 1:40-45; Matthew 8:2-4; Luke 5:12-16
-The man borne by four, of palsy: Mark 2:3-12; Matthew 9:1-8: Luke 5:17-26
-The impotent man who had been afflicted thirty-eight years: John 5:1-16
-The man with withered hand: Mark 3:1-5; Luke 6:6-10; compare Matthew 12:9-13
-The centurion's servant, of palsy: Matthew 8:5-13; Luke 7:1-10
-The woman who had been twelve years afflicted with issue of blood: Mark 5:25-34; Luke 8:43-48; Matthew 9:20-22
-Sight restored to two men: Matthew 9:27-31
-Hearing and speech restored to a man: Mark 7:32-37
-Sight restored to a man: Mark 8:22-26
-Sight given to a man who was born blind: John 9
-A woman who had been eighteen years afflicted: Luke 13:11-17
-A man, of dropsy: Luke 14:1-6

-Ten men, of leprosy: Luke 17:11-19
-Sight restored to a beggar: Luke 18:35-43; compare Matthew 20:29-34
-Sight restored to Bartimaeus: Mark 10:46-52; compare Matthew 20:29-34
-The ear of Malchus [or Marcus], the high priest's servant: Luke 22:50-51

## MIRACLES OF SUPPLY

-Water converted into wine: John 2:1-11
-Peter's net filled with immense catch of fish: Luke 5:1-11
-Five thousand men, besides women and children, fed: Matthew 14:15-21; Mark 6:35-44;
 Luke 9:12-17; John 6:5-14
-Four thousand men, besides women and children, fed: Matthew 15:32-39; Mark 8:1-10
-A fish furnishes tribute money: Matthew 17:27
-A great haul of fish: John 21:6-14

## MIRACLES OF JUDGMENT

-The swine run down a steep place into the sea, and are drowned: Matthew 8:30-32
-The fig tree withered: Matthew 21:18-21; Mark 11:12-14,20-24

## MIRACLES OF DELIVERANCE

-He delivers Himself from His enemies: Luke 4:30
-The wind and sea obey His word: Mark 4:37-41; Matthew 8:23-27; Luke 8:22-25
-Peter saved, trying to walk on the sea, as Jesus was walking: Matthew 14:28-31; Mark 6:45-52
-The wind ceases, and the vessel is instantly at the land: John 6:21; Mark 6:51-52
-Those sent to apprehend Him fall backward: John 18:4-6

## MIRACLES NOT DONE BY CHRIST, BUT TO ATTEST HIS DIVINITY

-The guidance of the Magi by a star to Bethlehem: Matthew 2:1-9
-The signs at His baptism: Matthew 3:16-17; Mark 1:9-12; Luke 3:21-23
-The signs at His transfiguration: Matthew 17:1-14; Luke 9:28-37; Mark 9:1-14
-The answer to His prayer: John 12:28-30
-The signs at His death: Matthew 27:45-53
-The signs at His resurrection: Matthew 28:2; Mark 16:4
-The signs at His ascension: Mark 16:19; Luke 24:50-51; Acts 1:6-12

2. If you completed assignment #1 above you have studied all the miracles Jesus used to accompany His teaching. Now read through the books of Matthew, Mark, Luke, and John and study the other general principles and teaching methods of Jesus. Record examples you find on the following chart:

Authority: Examples In....

Matthew                    Mark                    Luke                    John



Love and Compassion: Examples In....

Matthew                    Mark                    Luke                    John



Association And Imitation:  Examples In....

Matthew                    Mark                    Luke                    John



Response:  Examples In....

Matthew                    Mark                    Luke                    John



Delegation:  Examples In....

Matthew                    Mark                    Luke                    John



Environment:  Examples In....

Matthew                    Mark                    Luke                    John

**Visual Demonstration:**    Examples In….

Matthew                    Mark                        Luke                        John


**The Principle Of Gradual Learning:**    Examples In….

Matthew                    Mark                        Luke                        John


**Grouping Of Students:**    Examples In….

                    Matthew            Mark                Luke                John


**Individuals**


**Small Groups**


**Large Crowds**

# CHAPTER SIX

## A TEACHER COME FROM GOD:  THE METHODS - PART II

**OBJECTIVES:**

Upon completion of this chapter you will be able to:

- Briefly summarize how Jesus used the following teaching methods:

    - Known To Unknown
    - General To Specific
    - Object Lessons
    - Questions And Answers
    - Parables
    - Case Histories
    - Use Of Scripture
    - Contrasts
    - Problems
    - Occasions

**KEY VERSE:**

> **And when He was come into His own country, He <u>taught</u> them in their synagogue, insomuch that they were astonished, and said, Whence hath this man this <u>wisdom</u>, and these <u>mighty works</u>?  (Matthew 13:54)**

## INTRODUCTION

Most of the teaching of Jesus was verbal.  There is only one record of Him writing His message (John 8:6).  This chapter focuses on specific methods of verbal instruction used by Jesus.

## KNOWN TO UNKNOWN

Jesus used the known to teach the unknown.  He used the old to introduce the new.  He started with truths people knew and understood, then built on them to teach truths they did not know.

For example, Jesus would often state a truth from Old Testament law, then reveal a new truth.

(See Matthew 5:17-48).

Teaching must result in understanding. Revealing new truths by building on what is already known by the listener is an excellent way to achieve this goal. It is important that people understand with their minds the message because...

**For as he thinketh in his heart, so is he... (Proverbs 23:7)**

## GENERAL TO SPECIFIC

God reveals knowledge in ever increasing revelation. He moves from general to specific knowledge. A general revelation is made, then specific detail is added. For example, the first general prediction of a Savior was given in Genesis 3:15. Later on, as the Old Testament prophets wrote, God revealed much more detail concerning the coming Savior.

In John 6:35 Jesus revealed the general truth that He was the bread of life. In John 6:51-58 Jesus expanded this truth. He gave more detail about His body as the bread of life of which one must partake if they are to experience eternal life. Jesus used this pattern of teaching, which is a sound principle of learning you can follow.

## OBJECT LESSONS

Jesus used common objects and symbols with which His listeners were familiar to teach Biblical truths. He used the lilies of the field and the birds to teach God's care (Matthew 6:26-30). He used fishing and harvesting to illustrate the need for laborers to reach the unsaved (John 4:35 and Matthew 4:19).

Jesus used broken bread as a symbol for His broken body and wine as a symbol of His blood (Luke 22:19-20). He used the washing of the disciples' feet to illustrate humble service in leadership (John 13:1-17). Jesus called a little child as an example of the humility and trust required to enter the Kingdom of God (Mark 10:13-16). He used many symbols to illustrate the Kingdom of God, including the parables of the net, seeds, tares and wheat, leaven, mustard seed, etc.

When object lessons are used, they must be common objects or symbols with which the student is familiar.

## QUESTIONS AND ANSWERS

Jesus used questions and answers often in His teaching. Many times, Jesus would ask a question to make His listeners think. Sometimes He would require an answer (Matthew 16:13-16). Other times Jesus would ask a question which remained unanswered. It was designed only to make His listeners think and draw their own conclusions (Luke 10:25-37; Mark 10:17-

18).

Sometimes His questions were in the form of a problem to think about (Matthew 21:25-27). Other times He would ask a question to stimulate thinking (Matthew 5:13). Sometimes His entire conversation was a series of questions (Matthew 16:9-12). Often Jesus responded to questions which people asked by asking another question (Matthew 9:14-15; 12:10-11; 15:1-3; 21:23-25).

Jesus used questions in different ways. You can use them in these ways also:

-To introduce a lesson: Matthew 21:28
-Following a lesson: Matthew 21:40
-To recall the known: Mark 2:25-26
-To touch the conscience of listeners: Matthew 23:17
-To create faith: Mark 8:29
-To clarify a situation: Mark 10:3
-To rebuke criticism: Mark 2:25-26
-Motivate further thought or research: Matthew 6:25-31
-Consider different actions: Matthew 9:5
-Gain understanding of students: Matthew 16:15

The teacher can:

-Ask questions of a whole class.
-Ask a question of one student.
-Write questions on study or test papers.

Students can:

-Ask questions of the teacher.
-Ask questions of each other.
-Raise questions out of their own research of God's Word.

Here are some suggestions to help you ask good questions:

-Ask one question at a time. More than one question is confusing to the student.

-After asking a question, be silent. Wait for the student to respond.

-Follow up a general question with more specific questions on the same subject.

-Respond to answers given by students. Discuss the answers. Do not embarrass a student who gives a wrong answer.

-Ask questions that are "open" rather than "closed." A closed question is one that calls for a simple "yes" or "no" answer. Closed questions do not encourage the student to further thought and study.   Here is an example of a closed question:

"Did Jesus die on the cross?"

This question calls for only a "yes" answer.  Here is an example of an open question:

"Why did Jesus die on the cross?"

This question calls for more than a "yes" or "no" answer.  It causes  students to think further about the death of Jesus.  They can respond with many answers:

"Because this was the purpose for which God  sent Him into the world."
"Because of His love for the whole world."
"To save people from sin."
"For our healing as well as our salvation."
"For my own personal sins."

Each of these answers can lead to further discussion of the death of Jesus on the cross.

The "For Further Study" section of this chapter provides opportunity for you to learn more about the questions of Jesus and how to use questions in your own teaching.

## PARABLES

A parable is a story which uses an example from the natural world to illustrate a spiritual truth. The actual meaning of the word "parable" is to "lay beside, to compare."  In parables, Jesus used a natural example and compared it to a spiritual truth.  A parable is an earthly story with a Heavenly meaning.

Jesus often used parables as a method of teaching:

**And with many such parables spake He the Word unto them, as they were able to hear it.  (Mark 4:33)**

Parables must be explained to be understood:

**But without a parable spake He not unto them: and when they were alone, He expounded all things to His disciples.  (Mark 4:34)**

On one occasion the disciples asked Jesus why He taught using parables.  He answered:

**...Because it is given unto you to know the mysteries of the Kingdom of Heaven, but to them it is not given. (Matthew 13:11) (See also Luke 8:10).**

People with spiritual minds understand spiritual parables. Those with carnal minds do not:

**But the natural man receiveth not the things of the Spirit of God: for they are foolishness unto Him; neither can he know them, because they are spiritually discerned. (I Corinthians 2:14)**

A spiritually minded man is one who has been born again spiritually. Study John 3 for an explanation of the "born-again" experience.

The parables Jesus taught concerned subjects familiar to His audience. When you teach, you can use the parables Jesus taught but you can also create modern parables on subjects familiar to your audience.

Because cultures differ, parables which are understood by people in North America may not be understood by people in Australia, Africa, Asia, Latin America, and Europe. Each different group of people should have parables which relate to their own experiences. For additional study on this subject of parables see the "For Further Study" section of this lesson.

## CASE HISTORIES

Like parables, case histories are stories which illustrate Biblical truths. But case histories are true stories which actually happened. For example, the story of Lazarus and the rich man was an actual case history. Both Lazarus and the rich man were real people.

You can use the case histories Jesus used to teach lessons. See the "For Further Study" section of this chapter for additional examples of case histories used by Jesus. You can also use modern case histories. Use examples from your own spiritual experience. Use case studies of modern spiritual leaders to illustrate Biblical truths.

## USE OF SCRIPTURES

At the time of the ministry of Jesus, only the Old Testament had been written. Jesus knew the Old Testament Scriptures and used them frequently in His teaching. Turn to the "For Further Study" section of this lesson and review some of the Old Testament quotations used by Jesus.

It is important that you use God's Word in your teaching because it is HIS Words that are most effective in accomplishing spiritual purposes:

**So shall my Word be that goeth forth out of my mouth: It shall not return unto me void, but it shall accomplish that which I please, and it shall**

**prosper in the thing whereto I sent it.  (Isaiah 55:11)**

## CONTRASTS

Jesus used many contrasts in teaching.  A contrast can be made when two things are opposite or different from each other.  For example, Jesus contrasted good and evil, light and darkness, the rich and poor to illustrate truths He was teaching.

Contrasts can be used to teach spiritual differences. You can create original examples of contrasts or use the ones Jesus shared with His students.  Study the contrasts used by Jesus in the "For Further Study" section of this lesson.

## PROBLEMS

Jesus used problems of everyday life to teach lessons.  Real thinking and learning often begins with a problem.  For example, the scribe had a problem wondering who had the right to forgive sins (Mark 2:7).

**The scribes and Pharisees had a problem about the association of Jesus with publicans and sinners (Mark 2:16).**

Jesus used each of these problems to teach important spiritual truths.  For other examples of the use of problems in teaching, see the "For Further Study" section of this chapter.

## OCCASIONS

Jesus used occasions which were part of the common circumstances of life to teach lessons. He used the occasion of the woman coming to draw water at the well to teach a lesson on living water (John 4).  When Jesus was criticized for eating a meal with the Pharisees, He used the criticism as an occasion to teach the parable of the two debtors (Luke 7:36-50).

See the "For Further Study" section of this chapter for other examples of the use of occasion as a teaching method.

# SELF-TEST

1. Write the Key Verse from memory.

_____

_____

Write a brief summary of the following teaching methods used by Jesus:

2. Known To Unknown:

_____

_____

3. General To Specific:

_____

_____

4. Object Lessons:

_____

_____

5. Questions And Answers:

_____

_____

6. Parables:

_____

_____

7. Case Histories:

_____

_____

_____

8. Use Of Scripture:

_____

_____

_____

9. Contrasts:

_____

_____

_____

10. Problems:

_____

_____

11. Occasions:

_____

_____

(Answers to self-tests are provided at the conclusion of the final chapter in this manual.)

# FOR FURTHER STUDY

The following activities will provide further study for each subject discussed in this lesson.

## KNOWN TO UNKNOWN

Study the following references where Jesus used the known to teach the unknown:

**Matthew:** 5:17-48; 12:3-8,38-42; 16:5-12

**Mark:** 2:23-28; 7:9-13; 8:17-21; 10:17-20

**Luke:** 4:16-21; 6:3-5; 11:29-32; 13:1-5,15-16; 24:44-48

**John:** 3:14-15; 5:33-36,46-47; 6:32-33; 7:21-24; 8:39-59; 10:34-38

## GENERAL TO SPECIFIC

One of the best examples of teaching from general to specific is found in John 6:35. Jesus explains the general concept of His death on the cross. He gives specific details in John 6:35-58. In Matthew Jesus gives general information on His death in Matthew 9:43-45, but the disciples did not understand. He explained more details in Matthew 18:31-34, and they finally understood when He completed teaching on the subject in Matthew 22:15-23.

Can you find other examples of how Jesus used this method in His teaching?

## OBJECT LESSONS

Study the following references where Jesus used objects or symbols to teach spiritual truths. Make a chart to identify the spiritual truth Jesus was teaching. The headings for your chart should be as follows:

| Object/Symbol | Reference | Truth He Was Teaching |
|---|---|---|

Use the following references to complete your chart:

**Matthew:** Fishing 4:19; salt 5:13; light 5:14-16; fowls 6:26; lilies 6:28-33; motes and beams 7:1-5; gates 7:13-14; wolves and sheep 7:15; fruit 7:16-20; two houses 7:24-27; foxes and birds 8:20; garments and wine 9:16-17; harvest 9:37-38; sheep and wolves 10:16; sparrows 10:29-31; yoke 11:28-30; seeds and soils 13:1-43; treasure 13:44,52; pearl 13:45-46; net

13:47-50; plant 15:10-14; weather 16:1-4; child 18:1-6; sheep 18:12-14; camel and needle 19:23-26; fig tree 21:18-22; stone 21:42-44; penny 22:15-22; gnats and camels 23:24; cups and platters 23:25-26; seplechure 23:27; sheep and goats 25:31-33; bread and wine 26:26-29

**Mark:** Fish 1:16-18; seed and soils 4; bread and dogs 8:25-30; salt 9:50; children 10:13-16; camel and needle 10:23-27; penny 12:13-17; bread and wine 14:22-25

**Luke:** Fish 5:9-10; garments and wine skins 5:36-39; trees 6:43-45; two houses 6:48-49; soils and seed 8; harvest 10:2; lambs and wolves 10:3; light 11:33-36; 11:39-40; platters and cups; graves 11:44; sparrows 12:6-7; ravens 12:22-24; lilies 12:27-31; weather 12:54-57; mustard 13:17-19; leaven 13:20-21; wars and towers 14:26-33; salt 14:34-35; sheep 15:1-7; silver 15:8-10; mustard seed 17:6; child 18:16-17; stone 20:17-18; penny 20:20-26; bread and wine 22:19-22; fig trees 21:29-33

**John:** Wind 3:8; water 4:13-14, 7:37-38; harvesting 4:35; light 8:12, 9:5, 12:46; shepherd 10; corn of wheat 12:23-24; fines and branches 15; woman giving birth 16:19-21; feeding sheep 21:15-17; washing feet 13:1-17

## QUESTIONS AND ANSWERS

Study the following references where Jesus used questions and answers as a method of teaching:

**Matthew:** 5:13,46,47; 6:25-31; 7:3,4,9-11,16,22; 8:26; 9:4,5,15,28; 10:25,29; 11:7-9,16; 12:4,5,11,12,26,27,29,34,48; 13:27,28,51; 14:31; 15:13,16,17,34; 16:3,8-11,13,15,26; 17:17,25; 18:12,33; 19:5,17; 20:6,13,15,21,22,32; 21:16,25,28,31,40,42; 22:12,18,22, 31,32,42-45; 23:17,19,33; 24:2,45; 25:37-39,44; 26:10,40,50,53-55; 27:46

**Mark:** 2:8,9,19,25,26; 3:4,23,33; 4:13,21,30,40; 5:30,39; 6:38; 7:18,19; 8:5,12,17-21,27,29,36,37; 9:16,19,21,33,50; 10:3,18,36,38,51; 11:3,17,30; 12:9-11,15,16,24,26,35,37; 13:2; 14:6,14,37,48; 15:34

**Luke:** 2:49; 5:22,23; 6:4,9,32-34,39,41,42,46; 7:24-26,31,42,44; 8:25,30,44; 9:18,20,25,41; 10:26,36; 11:5,6,11-13,18,19,40; 12:6,14,17,20,24-26,28,42,49,51,56,57; 13:2,4,7,15,16,18,20; 14:3,5,28,31,34;15:4,8;16:2,3,5,7,11,12;17:7-9,17;8:7,8,19,41;19:31; 20:3,4,13,15,17,23,24,41,44; 22:11,27,35,46,48,52; 23:31; 24:17,19,26,38,41

**John:** 1:38,50; 2:4; 3:10,12; 5:6,44,47; 6:5,61,62,67,70; 7:19,23; 8:10,43,46; 9:35; 10:32,34,36; 11:9,26,34,40; 12:27; 13:12,38; 14:9,10; 16:5,19,31; 18:4,7,11,23,34; 20:15; 21:5,15-17,22,23

# PARABLES

| Subject | Reference |
|---|---|
| The mote and beam | Luke 6:37-43 |
| The two buildings | Matthew 7:24-27; Luke 6:47-49 |
| Children in the marketplace | Matthew 11:16; Luke 7:32 |
| The two debtors | Luke 7:41 |
| The unclean spirit | Matthew 12:43-45; Luke 11:24-26 |
| The rich man's meditation | Luke 12:16 |
| The barren fig tree | Luke 13:6-9 |
| The sower | Matthew 13:3-8; Mark 4:3-8; Luke 8:5-8 |
| The tares | Matthew 13:24-30 |
| The seed | Mark 4:26 |
| The grain of mustard seed | Matthew 13:31,32; Mark. 4:31,32; Luke 13:19 |
| The leaven | Matthew 13:33; Luke 13:21 |
| The candle | Matthew 5:15; Mark 4:21; Luke 8:16; 11:33 |
| The net | Matthew 13:47,48 |
| The hidden treasure | Matthew 13:44 |
| The pearl of great price | Matthew 13:45,46 |
| The householder | Matthew 13:52 |
| The marriage | Matthew 9:15; Mark 2:19,20; Luke 5:34,35 |
| The patched garment | Matthew 9:16; Mark 2:21; Luke 5:36 |
| The wine bottles | Matthew 9:17; Mark 2:22; Luke 5:37 |
| The harvest | Matthew 9:37; Luke 10:2 |
| The adversary | Matthew 5:25; Luke 12:58 |
| The two insolvent debtors | Matthew 18:23-35 |
| The good Samaritan | Luke 10:30-37 |
| The three loaves | Luke 11:5-8 |
| The true shepherd | John 10:1-16 |
| The strait gate | Matthew 7:14; Luke 13:24 |
| The guests | Luke 14:7-11 |
| The marriage supper | Matthew 22:2-9; Luke 14:16-23 |
| The wedding garment | Matthew 22:10-14 |
| The tower | Luke 14:28-30 |
| The king going to war | Luke 14:31 |
| The lost sheep | Matthew 18:12,13; Luke 15:4-7 |
| The lost piece of money | Luke 15:8,9 |
| The prodigal son | Luke 15:11-32 |
| The unjust steward | Luke 16:1-9 |

| Subject | Reference |
|---------|-----------|
| The importunate widow | Luke 18:2-5 |
| The Pharisee and publican | Luke 18:10-14 |
| The servant's office | Luke 17:7-10 |
| The laborers in the vineyard | Matthew 20:1-16 |
| The talents | Matthew 25:14-30; Luke 19:11-27 |
| The two sons | Matthew 21:28 |
| The murderous husbandmen | Matthew 21:33-43; Mark 12:1-9; Luke 20:9-16 |
| The fig tree | Matthew 24:32; Mark 13:28; Luke 21:29-30 |
| The watching householder | Matthew 24:43; Luke 12:39 |
| The man on a far journey | Mark 13:34 |
| The character of two servants | Matthew 24:45-51; Luke 12:42-46 |
| The ten virgins | Matthew 25:1-12 |
| The watching servants | Luke 12:36-38 |
| The vine and its branches | John 15:1-6 |

Now create some modern parables:

1. Select a Biblical truth or lesson you want to teach.
2. Think of some situation, condition, or example the listener will understand.
3. Using this example, create a parable [story] which illustrates the Biblical truth you want to teach.

Remember: The parable must illustrate the truth to be taught. A story just for the sake of telling a story is not effective. It must relate to or illustrate God's Word.

## CASE HISTORIES

Study the following examples of case histories. Can you find others in the teaching of Jesus?

| Case History | Reference |
|--------------|-----------|
| John the Baptist | Matthew 11:7-19; Luke 7:24-25 |
| Lazarus and the rich man | Luke 16:19-31 |

Now create your own case histories. Think of some true event that has happened which illustrates a Biblical truth. For example, do you know someone who accepted Jesus just before they died in an accident? You could use their "case history" to illustrate a message on "Today Is The Day Of Salvation."

What personal experience have you had which illustrate Biblical truths? Tell your own personal "case history" (also called your personal testimony). Use the lives of great spiritual leaders in modern times as case histories. How did their lives demonstrate the truths of God's Word?

## USE OF SCRIPTURE

Study the following references where Jesus used <u>Scriptures</u> in His teaching:

| New Testament Occasion | Old Testament Reference Used |
|---|---|
| Matthew 4:4: | Deuteronomy 8:3 |
| Matthew 4:7: | Deuteronomy 6:16 |
| Matthew 4:10: | Deuteronomy 6:13 |
| Matthew 5:21: | Exodus 20:13; Deuteronomy 5:17 |
| Matthew 5:27: | Exodus 20:14; Deuteronomy 5:18 |
| Matthew 5:31: | Deuteronomy 24:1,3 |
| Matthew 5:33: | Leviticus 19:12; Numbers 30:2, Deuteronomy 23:21 |
| Matthew 5:38: | Exodus 21:24; Leviticus 24:20; Deuteronomy 19:21 |
| Matthew 5:43: | Leviticus 19:18 |
| Matthew 9:13, 12:7: | Hosea 6:6 |
| Matthew 11:10: | Malachi 3:1 |
| Matthew 13:14,15: | Isaiah 6:9,10 |
| Matthew 15:4: | Exodus 20:12; Deuteronomy 5:16 |
| Matthew 15:4: | Exodus 21:17; Leviticus 20:9 |
| Matthew 15:8,9: | Isaiah 29:13 |
| Matthew 19:4: | Genesis 1:27, 5:2 |
| Matthew 19:5: | Genesis 2:24 |
| Matthew 19:18,19: | Exodus 20:12-16; Deuteronomy 5:16-20 |
| Matthew 21:16: | Psalms 8:2 |
| Matthew 21:42: | Psalms 118:22 |
| Matthew 21:13: | Isaiah 56:7; Jeremiah 7:11 |
| Matthew 22:32: | Exodus 3:6 |
| Matthew 22:37: | Deuteronomy 6:5 |
| Matthew 22:39: | Leviticus 19:18 |
| Matthew 22:44: | Psalms 110:1 |
| Matthew 26:31: | Zechariah 13:7 |
| Matthew 27:46: | Psalms 22:1 |
| Luke 22:37: | Isaiah 53:12 |
| Luke 23:46: | Psalms 31:5 |
| Luke 4:18: | Isaiah 61:1,2 |
| John 10:34: | Psalms 82:6 |
| John 13:18: | Psalms 41:9 |
| John 15:25: | Psalms 35:19, 69:4 |

# CONTRASTS

Study the following references where Jesus used <u>contrasts</u> in His teaching:

**<u>Matthew</u>:**

Chapter 5-7  The Sermon on the Mount uses many contrasts.

| | |
|---|---|
| 9:12 | Whole/sick |
| 9:13 | Righteous/sinners |
| 9:16 | Old cloth/new cloth |
| 9:17 | Old wine/new wine |
| 10:26 | Covered/revealed |
| 10:27 | Darkness/light |
| 10:28 | Body/soul |
| 10:32-33 | Confess/deny |
| 10:34 | Peace/sword |
| 12:33 | Good tree/corrupt tree |
| 12:35 | Good man/evil man |
| 12:37 | Words that justify/words that condemn |
| 13:12 | Those who have/those who have not |
| 13:13 | Those who see and hear/those who do not |
| 13:30 | Wheat/tares; good/poor soils |
| 13:47-50 | Good/bad fish; wicked/just |
| 15:25 | Save life/lose life |
| 18:23-35 | Those forgiven/those not |
| 16:19-18:18 | Binding/loosing |
| 19:30 | First/last |
| 20:16 | Called/chosen |
| 20:25-28 | Minister/servant |
| 21:28-30 | Son who worked/son who did not work |
| 21:42 | Rejected stone/cornerstone |
| 23:11 | Greatest is servant |
| 23:12 | Exalted/abased |
| 23:24 | Gnat/camel |
| 23:25-28 | Outside and inside of platter |
| 24:40-41 | Those taken and left |
| 25:1-4 | Wise virgins/foolish virgins |
| 25:29 | Hath given/hath not taken |

## Mark:

| | |
|---|---|
| 2:17 | Whole/sick, righteous/sinner |
| 2:19-20 | Those who fast/those who do not |
| 2:21 | Old garments/new garments |
| 2:22 | Old wine/new wine |
| 2:27 | Sabbath for man/man for Sabbath |
| 3:4 | Do good or evil on Sabbath |
| 2:4 | Good ground/poor ground |
| 4:12 | Seeing and hearing/not seeing and hearing |
| 4:22 | Things hidden/things revealed |
| 4:25 | Hath given/hath not taken |
| 4:31-32 | Least seed/greatest plant |
| 4:40 | Fear/faith |
| 7:6-13 | Doctrine/traditions |
| 7:14-15 | Within/without |
| 8:33 | Things of God/things of men |
| 8:35 | Save life/lose life |
| 9:40 | Against us/for us |
| 9:50 | Good salt/bad salt |
| 10:43-44 | Greatest/least, Chief is servant |
| 11:27-33 | Baptism of John? Of Heaven or men? |
| 12:17 | Caesar/God |
| 12:27 | God of dead/God of living |
| 12:44 | Giving from abundance/giving from want |
| 14:38 | Spirit/flesh |

## Luke:

| | |
|---|---|
| 5:31 | Whole/sick |
| 5:32 | Righteous/sinners |
| 5:36 | New garments/old garments |
| 5:37-38 | New wine/old wine |
| Chapter 6 | Many contrasts in this chapter |
| 7:20-21 | John the Baptist/Jesus |
| 7:47 | Love much/little |
| 8:17-18 | Secret/manifest; hath/hath not |
| 9:24 | Gain life/lose life |
| 9:48 | Least/greatest |
| 9:56 | Destroy/save |
| Chapter 10 | How to act in cities where you are received/how to act when not received |
| 11:23 | With Him/against Him |
| 11:34 | Single eye/evil eye |

| | |
|---|---|
| 11:35 | Light/darkness |
| 11:39 | Outside clean/inside not |
| 12:2-3 | Covered/revealed |
| 12:8-9 | Confess/deny |
| 12:47-48 | Few stripes/many stripes |
| 12:51 | Peace/division |
| 13:9 | Good fruit/bad fruit |
| 13:30 | Last/first |
| 14:8-11 | Exalted/abased |
| 14:12-14 | Rich/poor |
| 14:30 | Start but cannot finish |
| 14:34-35 | Salt/salt with no savor |
| 15:4-10 | Lost/found |
| 15:11-32 | Good son/bad son |
| 16:10-12 | Faithful in least/faithful in much |
| 16:13 | Two masters |
| 16:15 | Esteemed of man, not God |
| 16:19-20 | Rich man/poor man |
| 17:33 | Seek life/lose life |
| 17:34-36 | One taken/one left |
| 18:10-14 | Contrast of two men praying |
| 19:12-27 | Contrast of how men used the talents |
| 19:46 | House of prayer/den of thieves |
| 20:17-18 | Rejected stone/cornerstone |
| 20:38 | God of dead/God of living |
| 21:1-4 | Gifts of the rich/poor |
| 22:25-30 | Greatest/least |
| 23:31 | Green tree/dry tree |

## John:

| | |
|---|---|
| 3:6 | Born of flesh/spirit |
| 3:12 | Earthly things/heavenly things |
| 3:17 | Not to condemn but to save |
| 3:19-21 | Light /darkness |
| 4:13-14 | Living/natural water |
| 5:24 | Death to life |
| 5:29 | Good/evil resurrections |
| 6:32-33 | Moses' bread/God's bread |
| 6:63 | Spirit/flesh |
| 7:18 | Our glory/His glory |
| 7:24 | Two judgments |
| 8:12 | Light/darkness |

| 8:23 | Of this world/not of this world |
|------|--------------------------------|
| 8:35 | The servant/the son |
| 8:47 | Hearing/not hearing |
| 9:39 | Blind/seeing |
| 10:1-18 | The good shepherd/the thief |
| 10:25-29 | My sheep/other sheep |
| 10:37-38 | Do works/do not works |
| 12:24-35 | Saves life/loses life |
| 12:35-36,46 | Light/darkness |
| 12:47 | Judging/saving |
| 13:16 | Servant/Lord |
| 14:12 | Works/greater works |
| 14:23-24 | Keeping/not keeping works |
| 14:27 | Peace of God/peace of world |
| 15:2 | Fruit bearing vines/non-bearing vines |
| 15:15 | Servants/friends |
| 15:19 | Of world/not of world |
| 16:20-22 | Sorrow turned to joy |
| 20:27 | Faithless/believing |
| 20:29 | Those who see and believe/those who do not see |
| 21:18 | Contrast of Peter when he was young and old. |

## PROBLEMS

Study the following references where Jesus used problems in His teaching:

| Persons | Their Problems |
|---------|----------------|
| The scribes (Mark 2:7) | Who can forgive sins? |
| Scribes and Pharisees (Mark 2:16) | The association of Jesus with publicans and sinners. |
| "They" (Mark 2:18) | Why the disciples did not fast |
| The Pharisees (Mark 2:24) | Sabbath observance. |
| The scribes (Mark 3:22) | How Jesus cast out demons. |
| His fellow-townsmen (Mark 6:2,3) | The sources of Jesus' power. |
| Scribes and Pharisees (Mark 7:5) | Why the disciples did not observe the traditions. |

| Persons | Their Problems |
|---|---|
| The Pharisees (Mark 8:11) | They wanted a sign. |
| Peter, James, John (Mark 9:11) | The coming of Elijah. |
| The disciples (Mark 9:34) | "Who is the greatest?" |
| John and others (Mark 9:38) | Tolerance of other workers. |
| The Pharisees (Mark 10:2) | Divorce. |
| The rich young ruler (Mark 10:17) | Inheriting eternal life. |
| James and John (Mark 10:37) | Sitting on his right and left hand. |
| Chief priests, scribes and elders (Mark 11:28) | The authority of Jesus. |
| Pharisees and Herodians (Mark 12:14) | The tribute to Caesar. |
| Sadducees (Mark 12:23) | The resurrection |
| A scribe (Mark 12:29) | The first commandment. |
| Peter, James, John and Andrew (Mark 13:4) | "When shall these things be?" |
| Some at Simon's dinner (Mark 14:4) | The waste of ointment. |
| The high priest (Mark 14:61) | Whether Jesus claimed to be the Christ. |

## OCCASIONS

Study the occasions of life Jesus used to teach lessons:

| The Occasion | Its Use | Reference |
|---|---|---|
| Finding traders in the temple | Cleansing the Temple | Matthew 21:12-13; Mark 11:15-17 |

| The Occasion | Its Use | Reference |
|---|---|---|
| Nicodemus came to Him | Teaching the new birth | John 3:1-21 |
| Meeting a Samaritan woman | Transforming a life | John 4:1-42 |
| The leper came to Him | Cleansing physical body | Matthew 8:1-4;<br>Mark 1:40-45;<br>Luke 5:12-14 |
| The bringing of a palsied man | Spiritual and<br>physical healing | Matthew 8:5-13;<br>Luke 7:1-10 |
| He saw a man lying at the pool<br>of Bethesda | Physical healing | John 5:1-9 |
| The murmuring of the Pharisees<br>at the disciples for plucking<br>corn on the Sabbath | Teaching the true<br>relation of man and<br>the Sabbath | Matthew 12:1-8;<br>Mark 2:23-28;<br>Luke 6:1-5 |
| "Seeing the multitudes" | Sermon on the Mount | Matthew 5 to 7 |
| Eating with Simon the Pharisee | The two debtors | Luke 7:41 |
| The coming of His<br>mother and brethren | Teaching the supremacy<br>of spiritual relationship | Matthew 12:46-50<br>Mark 3:31-35;<br>Luke 8:19-21 |
| The disciples' question,<br>"Why speakest thou<br>unto them in parables?" | Teaching concerning<br>the mysteries of the<br>Kingdom | Matthew 13:10-17 |
| The disciples request an<br>explanation of the<br>parable of the tares. | Teaching concerning<br>the sons of evil | Matthew 13:36-43 |
| "Why eateth your master<br>with publicans?" | Teaching concerning<br>the whole and the sick | Matthew 9:10-13 |

# CHAPTER SEVEN

## TEACHING AIDS

**OBJECTIVES:**

Upon completion of this chapter you will be able to:

- Define "teaching aids."
- Explain what audio-visual aids are.
- Explain the importance of audio-visual aids.
- Create audio-visual aids.
- Evaluate teaching aids.

**KEY VERSES:**

And He took a child, and set him in the midst of them: and when He had taken him in His arms, He said unto them.

Whosoever shall receive one of such children in My name, receiveth Me: and whosoever shall receive <u>Me</u>, receiveth not Me, but <u>Him that sent Me</u>. (Mark 9:36-37)

### INTRODUCTION

In this lesson you will learn about various aids which can be used when you teach. You may not have access to all of the teaching aids discussed in this chapter because of your geographic location or financial situation. Because Harvestime International Institute courses are used in many places, this chapter is included for those who do have access to such materials. We have also included suggestions for teaching aids you can use without cost or special equipment.

### TEACHING AIDS

A teaching aid is something that helps you teach a lesson. This is why it is called an "aid." A teaching aid may be an activity or project which helps students understand a certain Biblical truth. A teaching aid may also be an object which can be seen, heard, or touched. Such an object is called an "audio-visual aid."

The word "audio" refers to hearing. The word "visual" refers to seeing. An "audio-visual aid" is something that can be seen, heard, or touched and which aids in learning. Sometimes the aid is totally audio, such as a cassette recording or a record.

Sometimes it is totally visual, such as a picture which illustrates a truth. Other times, both audio and visual are combined in a teaching aid. An example of this would be a movie or video with sound.

## THE IMPORTANCE OF TEACHING AIDS

Teaching aids are important because seeing, hearing, and doing are the main ways we learn. Special studies have been done which reveal that we remember:

...10% of what we hear,
...50% of what we see,
...70% of what we do,
...and 90% of what we see, hear, say, and do.

Because of this, it is important that teachers combine audio, visual, and activity aids in teaching.

## TYPES OF TEACHING AIDS

Here are some aids you can use in teaching:

## COMMON OBJECTS:

You can use common objects in the environment to illustrate a lesson. Jesus used many such aids. He used flowers, candles, birds, fish, seed, wheat, children, and rocks to illustrate His lessons.

## PICTURES:

Sources include photographs, newspaper clippings, book and magazine pictures.

## SLIDES:

Slides are transparencies [negatives] of pictures which have been mounted in cardboard frames and can be projected on a wall or screen through a slide projector. There are many sets of slides available concerning various Christian topics. These come ready to show on a slide projector. Some slide sets are accompanied by audio tapes or records.

You can also make your own slides if you have the proper equipment. You would need a camera, film for taking pictures to be made into slides, and a slide projector to show the finished product.

## COMPUTER AND THE INTERNET:

There are many Bible teaching programs available for computer. There are thousands of web sites on the Internet. These are tremendous resources for aids in teaching.

## FILMS AND VIDEO-CASSETTES:

Films and video-cassettes are motion pictures with sound which require special projectors to be shown. There are many Christian films and video cassettes available or you might consider making your own film or video-cassette if you have the proper equipment to do so.

## RECORDS AND AUDIO-CASSETTES:

Records and audio cassettes are forms of magnetic tape which record sound. There are many music and teaching tapes available. You can also create your own cassette tapes if you have a cassette recorder.

## BIBLE RESEARCH MATERIALS:

Encourage students to use Bible concordances, dictionaries, atlases, word study books, and commentaries if they are available. They will learn more about the lesson you are teaching while developing valuable Bible study skills.

## OVERHEAD PROJECTOR:

The overhead projector is a machine that projects images created on clear paper called "transparencies." Maps, outlines, words to songs, and Scriptures can be put on transparencies and projected on a screen for viewing and study.

## PROJECTS:

Assign projects to students to reinforce what they have learned. They may draw a map or picture, build a model of something [like the Old Testament tabernacle], write a report, or create a chart or graph. Practical ministry projects can be included such as witnessing to others, visiting the sick, feeding the hungry, etc. Projects encourage students to "do the Word" instead of being hearers only.

## MAPS:

Maps help students understand the land where Bible events occurred. Students can study maps or draw maps relating to the lesson.

## STUDY TRIPS:

Study trips are another excellent teaching aid. Students can visit a Bible museum, a prison, rest home, etc., to learn more and/or apply what they have already learned.

## CHARTS AND GRAPHS:

Create a chart or graph to illustrate the lesson. The chart could list main points of the lesson or the Scripture memory verse. Graphs could be used to make comparisons.

## GAMES, PUZZLES:

An excellent idea for working with children is to create games and puzzles to reinforce teaching. For example, write each individual word of a Scripture text on separate cards and mix them up. Have students place them in correct order. This will aid in memorizing the verse.

## DRAMA:

Students can act out [dramatize] the Bible lesson that has been taught. To do this, students take the roles of different characters in the lesson and act out the Bible story.

## PUPPETS:

Puppets are another way of acting out Bible stories. Puppets are miniature figures of people and animals that can be used to dramatize stories. They can be created out of cardboard, cloth, and other materials.

## CHALKBOARD OR WHITE BOARD:

Chalkboards or white boards are boards covered with a special coating which enables you to write on them, erase it, and use the same surface again. The teacher can use the boards to write key phrases, verses, or outlines of the lesson. They can also be used to draw pictures and illustrations. Students may also use the boards for the same purposes as a learning activity.

## THE FLANNEL GRAPH BOARD:

The flannel graph is a board covered with a material called flannel which permits the placing and removal of flannel-backed figures. Publishers have produced flannel graph figures [words, verses, and pictures] to go with many Bible lessons. You can also create your own figures, paste flannel on the back, and use them on the flannel board.

## FLASH CARDS:

Flash cards are pieces of paper or cardboard which can be held in your hand and "flashed" before students as a learning aid. For example, you can create memory verse flash cards. One side can have the verse written out. The other side can have the Bible reference. When you flash the Bible reference, have the class say the correct verse. When you flash the verse for them to see, they must give the correct reference.

## SONGS:

Songs can be used as a teaching aid. Use a song that:

-Relates to the lesson you have shared.

-Calls for the type of response you have requested in the lesson. For example, calling for acceptance of the Gospel if that has been the subject of the lesson.

-Is in keeping with the spirit of the lesson: Happy and joyous or slow and worshipful.

## TESTIMONIES:

Testimonies by students or guests can be used to illustrate the lesson. For example, if teaching a lesson on deliverance, have someone testify concerning their own deliverance.

## MEMORIZATION:

Memorizing verses, stories, and facts are an excellent aid to help students remember Bible lessons.

## TESTING:

Students can be tested to reinforce learning. The test may be oral or written. After the test, review any materials with which students had difficulty.

## STORY-TELLING AND REVIEW:

When working with young children have them tell the story in their own words after the lesson. Adults can summarize a lesson. Review the lesson through discussion, questions and answers.

## SOURCES OF TEACHING AIDS

You can make some teaching aids yourself. Others can be purchased from stores. If you have no funds or access to such aids, use simple objects from your own environment or activities requiring no materials or cost.

Jesus had no money for equipment or material to create teaching aids, yet He used them frequently by selecting items from the natural environment to illustrate His lessons. You may also be able to borrow audio-visual aids and necessary equipment from members of your church, other churches, libraries, the local public school, or your denominational headquarters.

## EVALUATING TEACHING AIDS

Use the following checklist to evaluate teaching aids:

1. Does the aid or activity relate to the lesson? Does it help explain or present it more clearly?

2. Is it appropriate for the age level for which it is intended?

3. Is it worth the price if you are purchasing and/or the time and cost to make it if you are creating an audio-visual aid?

4. How does it contribute to achieving the objectives you have set for the lesson?

5. Is it clear and easy to understand?

Remember: Teaching aids are just that...aids. Do not depend upon them alone. Our confidence is in the Word of God used by the Spirit of God to do the work of God in the lives of students.

A good farmer uses the best tools he has to plant his fields. But he knows that it is the seed, not his tools, that brings the harvest.

# SELF-TEST

1. Write the Key Verses from memory.

   _____

   _____

   _____

2. What is a teaching aid?

   _____

   _____

3. What are audio-visual aids?

   _____

   _____

4. Why are audio-visual aids important?

   _____

   _____

5. What type of audio-visual aids did Jesus use?

   _____

   _____

(Answers to self-tests are provided at the conclusion of the final chapter in this manual.)

# FOR FURTHER STUDY

1. Create an audio or visual aid for a lesson you plan to teach.

2. Evaluate the aid you created by using the checklist provided in this lesson:

    1. Does the aid or activity relate to the lesson? Does it help explain or present it more clearly?

    2. Is it appropriate for the age level for which it is intended?

    3. Is it worth the price if you are purchasing and/or the time and cost to make it if you are creating an audio-visual aid?

    4. How does it contribute to achieving the objectives you have set for the lesson?

    5. Is it clear and easy to understand?

# CHAPTER EIGHT

## ANALYZING THE AUDIENCE

**OBJECTIVES:**

Upon completion of this chapter you will be able to:

- Define "audience analysis."
- Explain the importance of audience analysis.
- Summarize steps for audience analysis.
- Summarize characteristics of various age groups.

**KEY VERSES:**

But Jesus did not commit himself unto them, because He knew all men.

And needed not that any should testify of man: for He knew what was in man. (John 2:24-25)

## INTRODUCTION

Before you begin to teach it is important to analyze your audience, set objectives, and plan the lesson. This lesson explains how to analyze the audience. The following two chapters concern setting objectives and lesson planning.

## AUDIENCE ANALYSIS

The "audience" is the group of people you will teach. To "analyze" something is to study it in detail, to carefully examine its characteristics, to study the parts of a whole. To analyze an audience means to carefully study the characteristics of a group of people you plan to teach.

## THE IMPORTANCE OF ANALYZING

Analyzing an audience is important because learning is affected by many factors which include language, education, culture, physical abilities, spiritual maturity, sex, marital status, social and economic level, personal needs, and age.

If you do not analyze the audience you may be teaching above or below their educational level and/or their level of spiritual maturity. You may not use a language they understand. You may not relate lessons to their social and economic level or to their personal needs.

You cannot know everything about every person in the audience. But you can think about what the majority of your audience is like and ask the Holy Spirit to help you meet their specific needs.

Jesus understood His audience. He knew His listener's customs and lifestyle because He was one of them. Jesus also had divine knowledge of their needs:

> **But Jesus did not commit Himself unto them, because He knew all men.**
>
> **And needed not that any should testify of man: for He knew what was in man. (John 2:24-25)**

God can show you things about an audience but you can also develop some practical skills to help you in this area. The Apostle Paul did this:

> **But when Paul perceived that the one part were Sadducees, and the other Pharisees, he cried out in the council, Men and brethren I am a Pharisee, the son of a Pharisee; of the hope and resurrection of the dead I am called in question. (Acts 23:6)**

When Paul ministered to Jews, He emphasized His Jewish background. When he spoke to Romans and other nationalities, he changed his approach. Paul knew the importance of analyzing his audience, speaking to them in their own language, and using an approach with which they could identify:

> **But Paul said, I am a man which am a Jew of Tarsus, ...and I beseech thee, suffer me to speak unto the people...**
>
> **And when they heard that he spake in the Hebrew tongue to them, they kept the more silence, and he saith...(Acts 21:39 and 22:2)**

## HOW TO ANALYZE AN AUDIENCE

Here are some steps to help you analyze an audience you plan to teach:

1. Pray for God to reveal to you their spiritual, emotional, mental, physical, and material needs:

> **If any of you lack wisdom, let him ask of God, that giveth to all men**

**liberally and upbraidith not: and it shall be given him. (James 1:5)**

2. We are told to covet [seek] spiritual gifts (I Corinthians 12:31). Ask God for the spiritual gifts of word of wisdom and word of knowledge. These gifts provide divine knowledge into people and their problems combined with a word of wisdom to help them. The gift of discerning of spirits is also helpful. (For further study of these spiritual gifts, see the Harvestime International Institute course, *"Ministry Of The Holy Spirit"*).

3. Observe and associate with your students. You will learn much by watching and being with them. Read the Gospels and note how Jesus observed the behavior of His own disciples and how this affected His teaching.

4. If you are ministering in a nation different than your own, learn all you can about the people by asking questions, observing, and reading books about the culture.

5. If possible, visit the homes of your students. You will learn much by viewing their personal environment.

6. If you are ministering to children, get to know their parents. Ask the parents about special needs of the children and work with the parents in these areas.

7. Use the guide for audience analysis provided in the remainder of this lesson.

## A GUIDE TO AUDIENCE ANALYSIS

Use this guide to analyze your audience. Learning is affected by the following factors:

### LANGUAGE:

The student must understand the language in which the lesson is taught. Otherwise, a translator must be used.

#### Analyze Your Audience:

-Do they speak the same language you do?

-Are there those in the audience who do not speak your language? If so, a translator will be needed.

### EDUCATION:

The difficulty of the lesson must be adjusted to the educational level of the majority of the audience. Some students have had formal schooling and others have not. Some are slow learners and others learn rapidly.

## Analyze Your Audience:

-What is the general educational level of the students? Are they illiterate, primary, secondary, or college level?

-Do you have students with educational problems? If so, what are they and how will you deal with them?

## CULTURE:

Culture affects the learning process. The teacher must use examples understood in the culture. Culture affects how we think and how we perceive the world around us. People learn best when lessons are related to their environment. Culture determines appropriate response. For example, some cultures are very unemotional. Others are emotional. How students respond to the Gospel is often affected by their culture.

In some cultures it is not acceptable for a woman to teach a man or a man to teach a woman. Other cultures require teachers to receive approval of an elder or tribal leader before teaching. You may need to adjust your style of dress or appearance to be accepted.

It is important to understand and work within the culture, as far as possible, as long as it does not violate Scriptural principles or compromise the presentation of the Gospel message.

## Analyze Your Audience:

-What cultures are represented?
-In what ways will the culture affect your method of teaching?
-How will the culture affect the application of your lesson?
-In what way will culture affect the response from students?
-Will you need to adjust your style of teaching or appearance to be accepted in this culture?

## PHYSICAL ABILITIES:

Physical abilities can affect learning. For example, a teacher of students who cannot hear or see will have to adjust their methods of instruction.

## Analyze Your Audience:

-Move those with vision and hearing problems to the front.
-Make sure visual aids are large enough to be seen.
-Use an interpreter for the deaf [sign language], if possible.

-You may need to arrange special assistance for those with other physical handicaps.
-Minister God's healing power to them.

## SPIRITUAL MATURITY:

Your audience can consist of unbelievers, new believers, mature believers or a mixture of all three. Paul warns that some people are not ready for "the meat of the Word" [deeper spiritual truths]. People must be fed "the milk" of the Word [basic truths] before moving on to deeper Biblical subjects (I Corinthians 3:1-2).

### Analyze Your Audience:

-Will it be mostly unbelievers? This would probably be true in an open air meeting or city-wide crusade. Your message should target unbelievers.

-Is the audience mostly new believers? If so, they will need instruction in basic principles of faith.

-Will it be mostly believers? This might be true of a retreat or special meeting open only to church members. But never assume everyone is a believer. Always give opportunity for people to repent and accept Jesus as Savior.

-What do you know about their spiritual level of maturity?

## SEX:

Whether an audience is all male or all female or mixed sexes can affect teaching. For example, a lesson on the Biblical responsibility of husbands to love their wives would be more appropriate for a male audience than a female audience.

### Analyze Your Audience:

-Will it be all male?
-Will it be all female?
-Will it be mixed sexes?

## MARITAL STATUS:

Married couples have different problems and needs than do single people, divorced, and widowed. People with children face some challenges that childless couples do not.

## Analyze Your Audience:

Analyze your audience to determine how many are:

-Single
-Married with children
-Married without children
-Widowed with children
-Widowed without children
-Divorced and not remarried, raising children alone
-Divorced and not remarried, no children
-Divorced and remarried, no children
-Divorced and remarried with children

## SOCIAL AND ECONOMIC LEVEL:

Adjust your teaching to the economic and social level represented by a majority of the audience. Jesus ministered differently to the woman at the well (John 4) than He did to Nicodemus (John 3). The woman was of a lower economic class. Nicodemus was from the upper class.

Paul said we must be willing to adjust in order to communicate the Gospel:

> **...I am made all things to all men, that I might by all means save some.
> (I Corinthians 9:22)  (See also verses 19-21).**

## Analyze Your Audience:

-What is the general economic level?  Are they upper class, middle class, lower class?  Do they have great financial needs?

-What are the occupations?  Students, ministry, business and professional workers, retired, housewives, laborers, unemployed?

-Where do they live?  Cities, villages, remote areas, poor areas, middle or upper class areas.  Are they migrant [move frequently]?  Are they homeless?

## PERSONAL NEEDS:

It is important to know the physical, mental, spiritual, emotional, and material needs of an audience.  This is vital in gaining attention, application and in calling for response.

## Analyze Your Audience:

Here are some common human needs and problems:

-Spiritual Needs:

      -Salvation
      -Assurance of salvation
      -Sanctification/holiness
      -Water baptism
      -Baptism of the Holy Spirit
      -Healing and deliverance
      -Spiritual maturity: For example, gifts of the Spirit, fruits of the Spirit, knowing God's will, dealing with life crises, dealing with temptation, warfare, prayer, being spiritually reproductive, etc.

-Emotional Needs:

      -Fear
      -Loneliness
      -Depression and discouragement
      -Bitterness
      -Unforgiveness
      -Self-concept
      -Anger, temper, other disposition problems
      -Hatred
      -Guilt
      -Jealousy
      -Rebellion

-Financial Needs:

      -Insufficient money to meet basic needs
      -Needs employment

-Physical Needs:

      -Illness
      -Weight problems
      -Appearance problems

-Special Problems:

    -Divorce
    -Suicide tendencies
    -Immorality
    -Abortion
    -Drugs
    -Cigarettes
    -Alcohol
    -Occult
    -Prejudice
    -Demon oppression/possession
    -Grief/dealing with death
    -Gossip, complaining, cursing, profanity
    -False cults
    -Bad habits and practices
    -Training of children

## AGE:

The content and difficulty of a lesson must be adjusted to the age level of the students. Attention span and ability to learn varies from age to age. People who have studied how people grow and develop mentally, physically, socially, and spiritually have identified various characteristics for different age groups. These characteristics or qualities are general traits that apply to students in a certain age group. The qualities may differ from culture to culture:

### Ages 2-3:

A. Physically:

    1. Imitates; likes to help.
    2. On the move; needs both physical activity and rest periods.
    3. Has low endurance, a sensitive nervous system.
    4. Likes to handle things; is very curious.
    5. Likes rhythm and rhyme.
    6. Cannot co-ordinate smaller muscles. Large muscles are developing.
    7. Grows and learns as he plays.

B. Mentally:

    1. Is imaginative.
    2. Attention span, 3 to 4 minutes.
    3. Likes the familiar and repetition.

4. Has limited vocabulary; likes simple stories.
5. Learns through senses of seeing, hearing, touching, smelling, tasting.
6. Interrupts stories; can sing easy songs.
7. Absorbs details.
8. Believes what he is told.
9. Does not learn well by direct exhortation.
10. Is developing an individual personality.
11. Is sensitive to other's emotions.

C. Socially:

1. Is timid, afraid of crowds.
2. Has imaginary fears.
3. Needs individual attention.
4. Plays alone. Must learn to play with others.
5. Is selfish; has to learn to share and help.
6. Likes to play stories, act out parts.
7. Is an imitator.
8. Needs consistent discipline.
9. Tires easily; is upset by confusion.
10. Desires to please parents or teacher.
11. Needs love, understanding, and security.

D. Spiritually:

1. Is able to understand how to thank and please God; that the Bible is God's Book; that the church is God's house.
2. Thinks of God as a real and loving person.
3. Learns of God through nature and common experiences in which God is mentioned.
4. Needs to feel that his teacher and God love him.
5. When properly taught, trustfully depends on the Lord.
6. Prays when motivated emotionally.
7. Learns to give because he loves Jesus.

## Ages 4-5:

A. Physically:

1. Is capable of more self-care.
2. Can dress himself.
3. Likes physical activity.
4. Talks a lot.
5. May have temper tantrums.

106

6. Muscles still developing.
7. Has slight physical endurance.

B. Mentally:

1. Can take a program that is not too varied.
2. Has an attention span of about 10 minutes.
3. Imagination is good.
4. Understands little about time and space.
5. Easily aroused to love and sympathy.
6. Increasing in mental ability.
7. Realistic
8. Can memorize short verses.
9. Ready to meet new emotional and intellectual experiences.

C. Socially:

1. Ready to meet new social experiences.
2. Good at certain play skills.
3. Growing in ability to get along with others.
4. Likes to play games involving co-operation.
5. Better disciplined.
6. Self-centered; needs practice in sharing and giving.
7. Growing in friendliness.
8. Developing leadership qualities.
9. Loves intensely and desires to please.
10. Likes to act out or play the stories.

D. Spiritually:

1. Can sincerely worship the Lord; can be led to appreciate God through His wonders in nature.
2. Speaks of the Lord in a personal way.
3. Understands that God loves and cares for him.
4. Knows that willful disobedience is sin.
5. Can learn the reality of God's presence, concern, guidance, provision, wisdom.
6. Is naturally trustful, but must be taught to trust and obey the Lord.

## Ages 6-8:

A. Physically:

1. Rate of growth slows down.

2. Has sudden bursts of energy.
3. Tires easily.
4. Needs varied activities.
5. Needs to learn to finish what he starts.
6. Likes to handle objects.

B. Mentally:

1. Excitable and sympathetic.
2. Likes special affection and guidance.
3. Imaginative, reasoning.
4. Learns through the senses, experience, and words.
5. Likes Bible stories that show God's power.
6. Likes to solve mental problems verbally.
7. Learns to choose.
8. Memorizes words easier than thoughts.
9. Begins to appreciate geographical and historical backgrounds.

C. Socially:

1. Grows under praise for right actions.
2. Needs practice in helpfulness, kindness, co-operation, unselfishness, consideration.
3. Imitates adults and wants adult approval.
4. Enjoys stories about children his own age.
5. Sometimes rebellious; tells tall tales.
6. Prefers non-competitive group activities.
7. Chooses friends; changes best friend often.

D. Spiritually:

1. Profits by spiritually mature examples.
2. Able to realize God's love and forgiveness.
3. Learns reverence by precept and example.
4. Often is ready to accept Christ as Savior.
5. Can learn to pray and live for Jesus.
6. Can solve problems by going to the Bible.
7. Needs to be taught to confess sin promptly.
8. Is curious about death.
9. Likes action and missionary stories.

## Ages 9-11:

A. Physically:

1. Is in healthiest state of life.
2. Is active and exuberant.
3. Growing in independence.
4. Is not too tidy.
5. Likes outdoor activities.
6. Grows moderately.

B. Mentally:

1. Can use Bible to find references and solutions to problems; also maps and dictionaries.
2. Has good memorizing ability; is alert and critical of own work.
3. Is developing concepts of time and space.
4. Is interested in problems.
5. Is eager for information; is active.
6. Has many interests; can write poems, stories.
7. Is creative if you give him your time, interest, and understanding.
8. Likes to check own progress.
9. Is interested in nature and courageous people.
10. Has increased power of concentration.

C. Socially:

1. Can be encouraged to have high standards.
2. Interested in fairness.
3. Likes to participate in class.
4. Prefers own pals; dislikes opposite sex.
5. Has group loyalty.
6. Admires leaders.
7. Should be taught respect for authority.
8. Is less shy than when younger.

D. Spiritually:

1. Ready for salvation.
2. Responds to teaching on growing in Christ.
3. Can understand doctrinal truths.
4. Needs encouragement on daily devotions.
5. Can be interested in winning those in own family and neighborhood.

## Ages 12-14:

A. Physically:

1. Grows fast and unevenly.
2. Girls mature earlier than boys.
3. Embarrassed by clumsiness which is caused by uneven growth.
4. Spurts of energy and slumps of fatigue.
5. Often most difficult period of life.

B. Mentally:

1. Has keener mind; can memorize well if interest is aroused.
2. Has strong sense of humor.
3. Daydreams, fancying himself a hero.
4. Over-responds emotionally.
5. Wants to make own life-decisions.
6. Is sensitive, frank, subject to extreme moods, critical, rebellious.

C. Socially:

1. May transfer loyalty from home to school, teacher, or some person he idealizes.
2. Follows the crowd.
3. Hungers for "experiences"; puts on front of indifference.
4. Dreads being considered childish; tries to act adult.
5. Beginning to be attracted to opposite sex.
6. Craves to be important, win friends and be one of the gang.

D. Spiritually:

1. Looks to older young people for leadership.
2. Is in questioning stage.
3. Must recognize need of a Savior and have assurance of salvation.
4. Needs guidance.

## Ages 15-18:

A. Physically:

1. Outgrowing their physical awkwardness.
2. Forming and stabilizing physical habits.
3. Care about their personal appearance.
4. Are attracted to the opposite sex.

B. Mentally:

1. Have developed reasoning powers.

2. Remembers ideas more often than words.
3. Idealistic and often creative.
4. Controls imagination with reason and judgment.

C. Socially:

1. Likes organization and leadership responsibility.
2. Wants to belong to a group.
3. Desires the approval of others their own age.
4. Wonders about the future.
5. Have an increased desire to help others.
6. Struggles to control their emotions.
7. Looks for thrills.
8. Prone to be moody.
9. Rebels against authority.
10. Longs for security.

D. Spiritually:

1. Often has doubts about spiritual things.
2. Responds quickly to emotional appeals.
3. Wants a personal, active Christianity that "works."

## Adults:

A. Physically:

Physically adults have reached maturity in size and stature. They have the physical ability to sit still longer than young children. Older adults may struggle with health problems more than younger adults. Adults may be concerned about their physical appearance and abilities if they do not conform to what is considered normal in their culture.

B. Mentally:

Mental abilities, attitudes and values have been firmly instilled. Adults are more "set in their ways" and it is harder for them to change. Generally, it seems to grow more difficult to learn new things as age increases. Attention span is better in adults than children. They can take a longer lesson and a more varied approach. Most adults have a good understanding of their language and culture. Most adults prefer learning concepts to memorizing facts.

C. Socially:

Most adults have usually settled in a certain social and economic level. The majority of their friends will usually be from the same level. Some may be struggling to improve their social and economic status. Most have chosen or will shortly choose their mates.

D. Spiritually:

Adults need spiritual guidance in major life decisions such as marriage, ministry, higher education, and occupational choices. They also need guidance in couple and family relationships.

Believers need further instruction in spiritual maturity and to become actively involved in the ministry of the church. They need to discover and use their spiritual gifts. Unbelievers need to hear the Gospel and be brought to salvation.

# SELF-TEST

1. Write the Key Verses from memory.

_____

_____

2. What is meant by "audience analysis"?

_____

3. Why is audience analysis important?

_____

4. Summarize steps in analyzing an audience.

_____

_____

5. Select a certain age group you already teach or plan to teach. Review the characteristics for that age group in this lesson. Write a summary about the age group.

_____

_____

_____

(Answers to self-tests are provided at the conclusion of the final chapter in this manual.)

## FOR FURTHER STUDY

1. Jesus had twelve disciples.  Using the skills you learned in this chapter, analyze this audience.  You will find the information on the twelve disciples in Matthew, Mark, Luke, John and the book of Acts.

2. Analyze an audience you plan to teach.

3. Study the lessons taught by Jesus to Nicodemus in John 3 and to the woman at the well in John 4.  One was upper class and intelligent.  One was lower class.  How did the teaching methods and lesson content differ?  How were they alike?

# CHAPTER NINE

## STATING OBJECTIVES

**OBJECTIVES:**

Upon completion of this chapter you will be able to:

- Define the word "objective."
- Explain the importance of objectives in teaching.
- Write objectives.
- Use a checklist to evaluate objectives.
- Explain the difference between general and specific objectives.
- Identify the final goal of Biblical teaching.

**KEY VERSE:**

**Whom we preach, warning every man, and teaching every man in all wisdom: that we may present every man perfect in Christ Jesus. (Colossians 1:28)**

## INTRODUCTION

You have learned that true spiritual growth is not measured by what a student hears, but by what he does about what he hears. In this chapter you will learn how to state objectives which will help you determine if students have really understood and are acting upon what they have learned.

## OBJECTIVES

An objective is an aim or end of an action. It is a point, goal, or desired outcome to be achieved. When a teacher states objectives, he writes statements of goals for his students. These are stated in terms which describe what the students will be able to do after completing the lesson. The lesson you are currently studying has objectives. Go back to the beginning of the lesson and review these objectives.

## THE IMPORTANCE OF OBJECTIVES

Objectives are important because:

1. They direct the teacher's prayers, plans, teaching, and learning activities towards a specific goal. You know exactly what you want to accomplish in each lesson so you can pray, plan, teach and prepare learning activities accordingly.

2. They can be used to measure the effectiveness of teaching. You will be able to tell if students have really learned what you wanted to teach them.

3. They improve your teaching. Because you can measure the effectiveness of your teaching, you can tell when you fail and when you succeed. You can learn from both failure and success and continue to improve your teaching.

4. They help students become doers instead of only hearers of the Word. When you set objectives and communicate them clearly to students before you begin to teach, then they will know what is expected of them.

## HOW TO WRITE OBJECTIVES

## STATE OBJECTIVES IN TERMS OF STUDENT PERFORMANCE:

Say specifically what you want them to be able to do. Here is an objective stated in terms of student performance:

"Upon conclusion of this lesson the student will be able to explain John 3:16."

Here is an objective that is stated incorrectly:

"I will teach the students John 3:16."

The first objective is stated correctly because it identifies what you want the student to be able to do at the end of the lesson. You can determine if he has learned properly by asking him to explain John 3:16 to you.

The second objective is incorrect. It states what you will do rather than what you want the student to be able to do. How will you know you have properly taught him? The objective gives no way to determine this.

## BEGIN EACH OBJECTIVE WITH A VERB:

A verb is an action word that identifies what the outcome should be. Use an opening statement like this:

> "Upon completion of this lesson the student will be able to:"

Then list objectives, starting each one with a verb. In the "For Further Study" section of this chapter there is a list of verbs to help you in stating objectives. Here is an example of an objective started with a verb:

> "Upon completion of this chapter the student will be able to explain the plan of salvation."

"Explain" is an action word. It tells what you want the student to be able to do as a result of the lesson.

## STATE EACH OBJECTIVE INDIVIDUALLY:

State only one learning outcome per objective. Here are some examples:

> Upon completion of this chapter the student will be able to:
> Right: Quote John 3:16.
> Wrong: Quote and explain John 3:16.

If you want them to explain it also, you should state two separate objectives:

> Upon completion of this lesson the student will be able to:
> Quote John 3:16
> Explain John 3:16

## STATE OBJECTIVES IN SEQUENCE:

Each objective should relate to what precedes and/or follows it. For example, "quote John 3:16" is a good objective to list before "explain John 3:16." The student must know it to be able to explain it.

## STATE EACH OBJECTIVE IN TERMS OF BEHAVIOR YOU CAN OBSERVE:

Here are some examples:

> Upon completion of this chapter the student will:
> Right: Explain John 3:16.
> Wrong: Understand John 3:16

If the student can explain John 3:16 you will know he understands it. If your objective is stated "Understands John 3:16" it is not measurable. It does not state WHAT the student will do to enable you to know if you have met the objective.

## MAKE EACH OBJECTIVE ACHIEVABLE:

If you set objectives that are too difficult, students will become discouraged.

## CHECKLIST

Use this list of questions to check the objectives you write for your students:

1. Is it written in terms of student performance? Does it say what you expect from the student rather than what you will do?

2. Is it observable? Have you written the objective in terms of behavior you can observe to see if you have accomplished the goal?

3. Is it specific? Does it describe clearly and specifically what is expected of the student.

4. Is it individual? Is there just one learning outcome per objective?

5. Is it sequential? Does it relate to objectives which precede or follow?

6. Is it achievable? Make sure it is not too difficult for the student to achieve.

7. Is it Biblical?

## GENERAL AND SPECIFIC OBJECTIVES

You will set both general and specific objectives for your students.

## GENERAL OBJECTIVES:

General objectives are goals that apply to your teaching in general. They are objectives students should achieve over a period of time. Here are some general objectives that should be basic goals for each teacher. These objectives are set in terms of student behavior that you can observe:

As a result of the lessons I teach, the student will:

## Respond To The Gospel:

This objective is easily observed. Does the student repent and turn from sin?

## Receive The Baptism Of The Holy Spirit:

The teacher should help lead each student into this experience. The sign of speaking in other tongues and the evidence of power to witness can be observed to see if this goal has been achieved.

## Be Baptized In Water:

Students who have been born again should be encouraged to follow Jesus in this public confession of their faith.

## Demonstrate Spiritual Fruit:

An important objective of teaching the development of Christ-like character. This would include the spiritual fruit listed in Galatians 5:22-23. It would also include developing a Kingdom lifestyle based on the principles taught by Jesus and further expanded in the Epistles in the New Testament.

## Discover Spiritual Gifts:

The Bible reveals that each believer has at least one spiritual gift. It is the responsibility of the Christian teacher to help students discover their spiritual gifts.

## Use Spiritual Gifts:

It is not enough just to discover spiritual gifts. The student should be encouraged to use these gifts in the work of the ministry.

## Reproduce Spiritually:

The teaching cycle is not complete until the student that is taught reproduces spiritually. See II Timothy 2:2.

## Engage In Personal Bible Study:

Fostering personal Bible study is an important general objective. The way you teach the Bible should encourage students to study it on their own. The Harvestime International Institute Course, *"Creative Bible Study Methods,"* can help you  teach students various methods of personal Bible study.

Use Bible Research Materials:

If you have access to Bible research materials such as dictionaries, concordances, etc., students should be taught to use these materials.  The Harvestime International Institute Course, *"Creative Bible Study Methods,"* will help you teach students how to use such materials.

Pray Regularly:

Students should be taught how to pray regularly both in public and private.

Participate In The Church Fellowship:

Students should become active members of a local church fellowship.

## SPECIFIC OBJECTIVES:

Specific objectives are those you set for each individual lesson you plan to teach. These will vary from lesson to lesson, depending on the subject matter. Review the objectives stated at the beginning of lessons in this manual.  Observe how the specific objectives differ in each chapter depending on the lesson content.

## THE END GOAL

The Bible reveals the end goal, the final objective for all Biblical teaching:

**Whom we preach, warning every man, and teaching every man in all wisdom:  that we may present every man perfect in Christ Jesus. (Colossians 1:28)**

The final objective of teaching and preaching is to prepare students to stand before God perfected in Christ Jesus.

# SELF-TEST

1. Write the Key Verse from memory.

_____

_____

2. Define the word "objective."

_____

3. Why are objectives important in teaching?

_____

_____

4. What is the difference between general and specific objectives?

_____

_____

5. Which one of these objectives is stated correctly?

   On the conclusion of this lesson the student will:
   Example A:  Know John 3:16.
   Example B:  Recite John 3:16.

Example_____is correct.

6. What is the final goal in Biblical teaching?

_____

_____

(Answers to self-tests are provided at the conclusion of the final chapter in this manual.)

# FOR FURTHER STUDY

1. Use the following chart when selecting verbs to write objectives:

## EXAMPLES OF VERBS

| If the goal is: | Knowledge | Understanding | Skill |
|---|---|---|---|
| | Then use these verbs: | Then use these verbs: | Then use these verbs: |
| | name | analyze | help |
| | review | discriminate | guide |
| | list | between | teach |
| | state | compare | plan |
| | enumerate | differentiate between | ask |
| | recite | interpret | research |
| | recall | contrast | apply |
| | write | classify | internalize |
| | identify | select | produce |
| | memorize | choose | use |
| | trace | separate | practice |
| | become aware of | examine | solve |
| | become familiar with | discern | experience |
| | with | discover | explain |
| | define | match | communicate |
| | describe | reproduce | assist in |
| | recognize | organize | pray about |
| | label | interpret | show |
| | outline | evaluate | organize |
| | quote | locate | design |
| | summarize | discuss | demonstrate |
| | | | research |
| | | | develop |
| | | | study |

2. Write some specific objectives for a lesson you plan to teach. Use the checklist to evaluate the objectives you have written.

___1. Is it written in terms of student performance? Does it say what you expect from the student rather than what you will do?

___2. Is it observable? Have you written the objective in terms of behavior you can observe to see if you have accomplished the goal?

___3. Is it specific? Does it describe clearly and specifically what is expected of the student.

___4. Is it individual? Is there just one learning outcome per objective?

___5. Is it sequential? Does it relate to objectives which precede or follow?

___6. Is it achievable? Make sure it is not too difficult for the student to achieve.

___7. Is it Biblical?

3. Using the following outline to study the objectives God set for ministry gifts:

## EPHESIANS 4:11-16

A. The Varieties Of Ministry: Some apostles, some prophets, some evangelists, some pastors and teachers:

B. The Task: For the equipping of the saints, for the work of ministry, for building up the Body of Christ,

1. Desired Outcomes: Until we all attain to the unity of the faith and of the knowledge of the Son of God, to mature manhood, to the measure of the stature of the fullness of Christ;

2. Possible Attitudes: So that we may no longer be children,

(a) Undesirable: Tossed to and fro and carried about with every wind of doctrine by cunning of men, by their craftiness in deceitful wiles.

(b) Desirable: Rather, speaking the truth in love, we are to grow up in every way into Him who is the head, into Christ, from whom the whole body, joined and knit together by every joint with which it is supplied, when each part is working properly, makes bodily growth and builds itself in love.

# CHAPTER TEN

## LESSON PLANNING

**OBJECTIVES:**

Upon completion of this chapter you will be able to:

- Identify factors common to every teaching situation.
- Identify parts of a basic teaching plan.
- Summarize steps for planning a lesson.
- Plan a lesson.

**KEY VERSE:**

**A wise teacher makes learning a joy.  (Proverbs 15:2)   The Living Bible**

### INTRODUCTION

You have studied the message Jesus taught. You have learned teaching methods, how to use teaching aids, audience analysis, and how to state objectives.  Now you will combine all of these skills in this chapter as you plan a lesson.

### THE TEACHING SITUATION

When you plan a lesson, remember that every teaching situation involves the following common factors:

**DIVINE AGENTS:**

The Father, Son, and Holy Spirit are the divine spiritual agents behind Biblical teaching.  The Holy Spirit is the power which enables the teacher to teach and opens the understanding of the student. (Review Chapter Two).

**THE TEACHER:**

The teacher is the one who knows the truth to be taught:

**And He began to teach them many things. (Mark 6:34)**

(Review Chapters One and Two, "A Teacher Come From God").

## A STUDENT:

A student is a faithful man or woman who attends with interest to the lesson given. The student learns as he reacts to what he sees, hears, and understands:

**...Spake He [Jesus] the word...as they were able to hear. (Mark 4:33)**

The teacher must do more than teach Biblical facts. Facts alone are not meaningful. The student must understand and apply facts. In Matthew 13 in the parable of the sower, the seed which fell by the wayside was snatched away because the hearer did not understand (Matthew 13:19). Students must understand the meaning of what is taught in terms of their own personal experience. (Review Chapter Eight).

## LANGUAGE:

The language used to teach must be understood by the student or else a translator must be used. (Review Chapter Eight).

## ENVIRONMENT:

People learn best when the lesson is related to their environment. What they learn must be practical and apply to the problems they face in life. The message must minister to the needs created by their home, work, or ministry environments. (See Chapter Eight).

## LESSON:

The lesson to be communicated is God's Word, the Bible. The Bible is the basic book of instruction. Other books and materials may be used, but God's Word is the final authority. (Review Chapters Three and Four).

## OBJECTIVES:

Each lesson must relate to general and specific spiritual objectives. (Review Chapter Nine).

## METHODS:

Every lesson is taught by using methods. (Review Chapters Five and Six).

## AN EXAMPLE

Here is an example of the factors of a common teaching situation using John 4:

**Divine Agents**: Jesus spoke the message of God the Father, empowered by the Holy Spirit.

**Teacher**: Jesus.

**Student**: The woman at the well.

**Language**: Jesus spoke to her in a language she could understand.

**Environment**: The environment was Jacob's well. Jesus used the environment to present the lesson.

**Lesson**: God is spirit and those who worship Him must worship in spirit and truth. Jesus is the source of living water.

**Objectives**: To lead the woman to realize her real need was not for physical water but for the living water.

**Methods**: Jesus used a common object [water] as a teaching aid to attract attention. He used a common occasion [coming to draw water] as an opportunity to teach. Jesus used contrasts between natural water and living water. He used conversation, questioning, and reference to tradition. He quoted from the Old Testament and used the present situation to relate to the needs of the woman. He applied the lesson to her life and called for personal response.

## LESSON PLANNING

You are now ready to plan a lesson. Follow these steps:

### STEP ONE - Prepare Spiritually:

Prepare your heart:

> **The preparations of the heart in man and the answer of the tongue is from the Lord. (Proverbs 16:1)**

Prepare your mind:

> **If any of you lack wisdom, let him ask of God, that giveth to all men liberally and upbraideth not; and it shall be given him. (James 1:5)**

Pray that God will prepare the hearts of the students to receive the Word. Pray for yourself, that God will anoint and enable you to share His Word.

## STEP TWO - Study The Lesson:

Read the Bible text for the lesson. Read surrounding passages that give the background of the lesson. Meditate on the passage by slow, thoughtful repetition of reading. Study everything the Bible says on the subject on which you will teach. If you have Bible research materials such as a concordance, word study book, and commentaries, use these for further research:

**Study to show thyself approved unto God, a workman that needeth not to be ashamed, rightly dividing the word of truth. (II Timothy 2:15)**

As you study, write down important points and special thoughts the Holy Spirit brings to your mind. You will use these notes to develop an outline of the lesson.

## STEP THREE - Analyze The Audience:

Use the skills you learned in Chapter Eight of this course to analyze the audience you will teach.

## STEP FOUR - Set Objectives:

Using the study notes you have made and keeping in mind your audience analysis, set objectives for the lesson. (Review Chapter Nine of this course, "Stating Objectives").

## STEP FIVE - Outline The Basic Sections Of The Lesson:

There are four basic parts of a plan for teaching a Biblical lesson: The introduction, the body of the lesson, the application, and conclusion. An outline consists of brief written statements that summarize the important truths you want to present in each section of the lesson. An outline is a valuable teaching aid because it helps you stay on the subject as you teach. It also helps you remember important truths you need to teach students. Use the notes you took during your study to develop the teaching outline.

Here is the way to write an outline:

**Title**: Titles help people remember the subject. They also help the teacher be specific about the purpose of the lesson. Select a title for the lesson that reflects the central truth. Ask yourself, "What am I talking about in this lesson?" Write the title at the beginning of your outline.

**Introduction**: The introduction is the beginning of the lesson. It is important that the introduction interest the student or he may not continue to listen.

Jesus did not have a standard introduction. He secured the attention of His listeners by several methods. Sometimes He specifically called for it by saying "Verily, verily." When Jesus said "Verily, verily," it was the same as saying "Listen carefully...this is important!"

Jesus also gained attention by starting with a statement of interest to the person He was addressing. For example, He opened the conversation with the woman at the well in John 4 by asking for a drink of water:

> **There cometh a woman of Samaria to draw water: Jesus saith unto her, Give me to drink. (John 4:7)**

She had come to the well to draw water, so He started at her point of interest. The introduction led to a discussion of the spiritual lesson on living water.

If the audience was interested in the law of Moses, then Jesus used this subject for an introduction. If they were concerned about the Kingdom promised to Israel, He would open with a statement on this subject. When you begin a lesson with a statement which interests your listeners, it attracts their attention so you can share the Gospel.

Jesus also used common objects, questions and answers, parables, case histories, Scriptures, contrasts, and problems as introductions to secure attention. He used occasions which were part of the common circumstances of life. He started with what people knew to teach the unknown and led them from general to specific teachings.

An introduction should be:

-Brief: If it is too long, interest may be lost.

-Appealing: It must attract interest of audience; focus on some need or concern.

-Memorable: It should be such that listeners can easily remember it.

-Relevant: The introduction prepares for the truths you will teach and orients listeners to the main idea of the lesson.

Prepare an introduction that will gain the interest of your students. On your outline write out a summary of how you will introduce the lesson.

**Body**: The "body" of the lesson is the main content of the teaching. In the lesson Jesus taught the woman at the well, the body of His message focused on the living water. It revealed the source of living water, a contrast between living and natural water, the response necessary to receive living water, and the results of drinking of that living water:

-The Source:

> ...Jesus answered and said unto her, If thou knewest the gift of God, and who it is that saith to thee, Give me to drink: thou wouldest have asked of Him and He would have given thee living water... (John 4:10)

-Contrast Between Living and Natural Water:

> ...Whosoever drinketh of this water shall thirst again: But whosoever drinketh of the water that I shall give Him shall never thirst...
> (John 4:13-14)

-The Response Necessary:

She must drink of the water from the spiritual source:

> ...Asked of Him and He would have given thee living water...Whosoever drinketh of the water that I shall give Him shall never thirst...
> (John 4:10,14)

-The Results:

> ...Shall never thirst; but the water that I shall give him shall be in him a well of water springing up into everlasting life. (John 4:14)

Here is an easy way to organize the body of a lesson in an outline:

    I. First main point.

        A. Additional statement on the first main point.
           1. Subpoint
           2. Subpoint

        B. Additional statement on the first main point.
           1. Subpoint

        C. Additional statement on the first main point.

    II. Second main point.

        (List statements about the second main point as you did for the first main point.)

Be sure the points are organized in a logical order which follows the Scripture text for the lesson. The main points should relate back to the main idea and the subpoints should relate to their main points. Make good transitions between points by relating each point to the previous one. Continue the outline until you have covered all the main points of the lesson. The number of points you have will vary from lesson to lesson.

**Application**: When you relate the truths of God's Word to everyday life, it is called "application." You "apply" what you teach to real life situations. After a Biblical truth is taught, it must be applied to the life and ministry of the listener. It must answer this question: "How does this truth affect me?"

In the example of Jesus and the woman at the well, He taught her about living water and then applied the lesson. He told her that this living water could be in her and change her life. He showed her how she could worship the real God in spirit and truth.

Application can be made using any of the teaching methods you learned in Chapters Five and Six. Asking and answering questions is an excellent way to apply truths you have taught. Let the students make applications themselves also.

Applications should be drawn from real life experiences which illustrate the lesson. You can find such illustrations in the Bible, history, biographies of famous people, parables, hymns, by reading books, and through personal observation and experience. People learn best in the context of doing. Students must _do_ if they are to learn:

> **If ye know these things, happy are you if ye do them. (John 13:17)**
> **(Review James 5 also).**

"Doing" is application. The application of the lesson can include projects and activities to help students apply truths they have learned. In the teaching outline, write out how you will apply the truths you have taught. Include the methods and activities you will use.

**Conclusion**: The conclusion ends the lesson. The conclusion of the lesson should include a summary of the main points taught in the body of the lesson. A summary does not have to be a boring rehearsal of facts. You can use any of the methods you learned in Chapters Five and Six to review the lesson. You can include an illustration or quotation, ask questions or give specific direction. Review is important. Jesus often repeated spiritual truths. Use as much repetition as necessary to assure that students understand the lesson.

The conclusion should also include an opportunity for response from the student. When Jesus concluded lessons, He always called for response. At the well, Jesus told the Samaritan woman, "Go call thy husband." This call for response resulted in her confession of sin. It is not enough to just hear the Word. It is not enough just to know how it applies to our lives. We must respond to what we have learned.

Response is possible only when the truth relates to us. This is why the application part of the lesson is important. We must understand how a message applies to us in order to respond to it. Revelation requires response. Revelation without application is only information and information alone does not change lives. Even the fact that God has revealed Himself in the beauties of nature requires response from man:

**Because that which may be known of God is manifest in them; for God hath shown it unto them.**

**For the invisible things of Him from the creation of the world are clearly seen, being understood by the things that are made; even His eternal power and Godhead, so that they are without excuse. (Romans 1:19-20)**

Examples of responses to a lesson are accepting Jesus as Savior, coming for prayer to receive healing or the Baptism of the Holy Spirit, confession of a sin, and commitment to Christian service. A call for response must not be based on emotional appeal. Jesus made it clear that to respond to the Gospel would be costly (see Mark 8:34-35).

Decide how you will check to see if the objectives you set are accomplished. Will you test the students? Will you have them do a project or activity using what they learned? Write out a summary of how you will conclude the lesson. Remember to include a call for response. How do you want students to respond to the lesson you have taught?

## STEP SIX - Select Methods And Aids:

Select the methods you will use to teach the lesson. Here is a list of the methods you have studied from which to choose:

-Known to unknown
-General to specific
-Object lessons/visual demonstration
-Questions and answers/discussion
-Parables
-Case histories [illustrating what you are teaching]
-Use of Scripture
-Contrasts
-Problems
-Occasions

Be sure the methods you select are appropriate to the audience and to the lesson. Plan teaching aids to use with the lesson and activities which include student participation.

## STEP SEVEN - Organize Materials:

Organize the materials you need to teach the lesson. This will include your teaching outline, Bible, written materials for students, teaching aids, and any supplies you need for the activities you have planned.

# SELF-TEST

1. Write the Key Verse from memory.

_____

_____

2. What are the factors common to every teaching situation?

_____

_____

3. What were the four basic parts of a lesson plan discussed in this chapter?

_____         _____

_____         _____

4. List the steps of lesson planning discussed in this chapter.

Step One:_____

Step Two:_____

Step Three:_____

Step Four:_____

Step Five:_____

Step Six:_____

Step Seven:_____

5. Use the outline in the "For Further Study" section to plan a lesson.

(Answers to self-tests are provided at the conclusion of the final chapter in this manual.)

# FOR FURTHER STUDY

1. One of the main objectives in teaching is to lead students to accept Jesus Christ as their personal Savior. This objective is possible even with children. It is only necessary that a child is old enough to understand and make a decision.

-Biblical examples of children coming to God are Joseph, Samuel, Jeremiah, Daniel, John the Baptist and Timothy.

-Conversion occurs on a child's level:  Matthew 18:3

-Humility is a quality children have that makes it easier for them to accept the Gospel:  Matthew 18:4

-A little child can believe:  Matthew 18:6

-To cause a child to stumble spiritually is serious: Matthew 18:6,8

-A child is of great value to God:  Matthew 18:10

-Jesus was still talking about children when He spoke of the lost sheep which was found:  Matthew 18:12,13

-It is not the will of the Father that one child be lost: Matthew 18:14

2. Analyze the common factors in the teaching situation of Jesus and Nicodemus in John 3:

Divine Agent:

_____

Teacher:

_____

Student:

_____

Language:

_____

Environment:

_____

Lesson:

_____

Methods:

_____

3. Analyze the structure of some messages of Jesus recorded in the Bible. For each, consider these questions:

Introduction: What method did He use to secure attention? How did He introduce the teaching?

Body Of The Message: What were the basic truths He taught? What methods did He use to present them?

Application: How did He apply the Biblical truths to the lives of the listeners?

Conclusion: How did Jesus conclude the message? What response did He call for?

4. Use the outline on the following pages to prepare lessons to teach.

# OUTLINE FOR PLANNING LESSONS

**Title Of Lesson**: _____

**Scripture Text**: _____

**Audience:** Summarize what you know about the audience you plan to teach:

_____

_____

**Objectives:** Upon conclusion of this lesson the student will be able to:

_____

_____

_____

## Lesson Outline

**Introduction:** How I will begin the lesson:

_____

**Body:** (Outline major points).

_____

_____

_____

_____

_____

_____

**Application**: How I will apply this lesson to the lives of my students:

_____

**Conclusion:** Plan each of the following:

Lesson summary: How I will summarize the lesson:

_____

Evaluation: How I will evaluate students to see if objectives have been met:

_____

Call for response: What I will ask the students to do:

_____

**Teaching Methods**: Teaching methods I will use to teach this lesson:

(Here is a list of the methods you have studied from which you can choose.)

_____Known to unknown                      -Case histories
_____General to specific                    -Use of Scripture
_____Object lessons/visual demonstration    -Contrasts
_____Questions and answers/discussion       -Problems
_____Parables                               -Occasions

Other:_____

**Teaching Aids:** Teaching aids I will use to teach this lesson:

_____

_____

**Materials Needed:** Materials I need to take to class:

__Bible__Teaching __Teaching
Aids__Other:_____

# CHAPTER ELEVEN

## EVALUATION

**OBJECTIVES:**

Upon completion of this chapter you will be able to:

- Define "evaluation."
- Explain why it is important to evaluate teaching.
- List four methods of evaluating Biblical teaching.
- Identify reasons for problems in the teacher/learner situation.
- Recognize problems as opportunities instead of obstacles.

**KEY VERSE:**

> **That ye may approve things that are excellent; that ye may be sincere and without offence till the day of Christ. (Philippians 1:10)**

## INTRODUCTION

You have learned how to set objectives, plan, and teach a Biblical lesson using various methods. But how do you know if your teaching is effective? How do you know if spiritual objectives are met and the lives of those you teach experience help and change? The answer to these questions is found in evaluation.

## EVALUATION

Evaluation is the process of carefully examining something. When you evaluate your teaching you carefully examine results to see if your ministry is effective. It is important that you evaluate your teaching if you are to improve the gift God has given you. Paul said you are to develop your judgment...

> **That ye may approve things that are excellent; that ye may be sincere and without offence till the day of Christ. (Philippians 1:10)**

# THE BASIS OF EVALUATION

Evaluation in Biblical teaching is based on the following:

## OBJECTIVES:

You can evaluate teaching in terms of objectives. Were the objectives set achieved by the student? You should state objectives that are measurable so you can tell if they are achieved.

Jesus set objectives for His disciples and evaluated the results of their learning experience:

> **And He called unto Him the twelve, and began to send them forth by two and two...**
>
> **And the Apostles gathered themselves together unto Jesus, and told Him all things both what they had done and what they had taught. (Mark 6:7,30) (See also Luke 9).**

## TESTING:

A test is an examination which determines if a student has learned what has been taught. God teaches and tests us through life experiences. Jesus evaluated His disciples through testing:

> **When Jesus then lifted up His eyes, and saw a great company come unto Him, He saith unto Philip. Whence shall we buy bread, that these may eat?**
>
> **And this He said to prove him: for He Himself knew what He would do. (John 6:5-6)**

Formal tests may be written such as the "Self-Tests" in this manual. They may also be oral, where questions are asked verbally and students respond verbally. Informal testing occurs when students confront real life and ministry problems. How students respond in these situations is more important than their response to formal testing.

## RESPONSE:

Teaching is also evaluated by the response of students:

-Were students attentive to the lesson?

-Did they respond to the appeal given by the teacher? For example, if the call was for salvation did the unsaved respond? If the call was for healing or baptism in the Holy Spirit, was there response from students? Is spiritual growth evident in response to teaching? Remember:

Spiritual growth is not measured by what a student hears, but what he does about what he hears.

## TEACHER PERFORMANCE:

The performance of the teacher is also part of the evaluation process. Use the checklist in the "For Further Study" section of this lesson to evaluate your teaching.

## ANALYZING PROBLEMS

Do not be discouraged if evaluation reveals problems in your teaching. Identifying problems provides opportunity for you to correct them. Even Jesus experienced problems with His students in the teacher/learner relationship. Consider the following:

-Read Luke 9:54-56. When James and John saw Jesus rejected, they wanted to call down fire from Heaven and consume the people. They had totally missed the message of Jesus who said...

> **For the Son of man is not come to destroy men's lives, but to save them...**
> **(Luke 9:56)**

-When Jesus began to teach that He must die for the sins of mankind, Peter rebuked Him. Jesus had to correct him (Mark 8:31-33).

-Even though Jesus had given authority to cast out devils, the disciples failed in ministering to a demon possessed child (Mark 9:13-28).

-Read Mark 10:35-45. James and John asked Jesus if they might sit by Him in His coming kingdom. The rest of the disciples were displeased with James and John when they heard this. All of them had missed the message Jesus taught:

> **But so shall it not be among you: but whosoever will be great among you,**
> **shall be your minister:**
>
> **And whosoever of you will be the chiefest, shall be servant of all.**
>
> **For even the Son of man came not to be ministered unto but to minister,**
> **and to give His life a ransom for many. (Mark 10:43-45)**

-The disciples slept in the hour of Christ's greatest need and when He had asked them to pray (Mark 14:32-42).

-One disciple betrayed Jesus, one denied Him, and the remainder fled when He was arrested

(Mark 14:43-72).

-The rich young ruler rejected the call of Jesus to discipleship (Mark 10:17-22).

Since Jesus was without sin, problems in His teacher/learner relationship did not rest with Him. The problem was with the students. God does not fail. His Word does not fail. Jesus does not fail. When there are problems in our teacher/learner situations there are only two areas to examine. The problem either rests with the teacher or with the learner.

Here are some common reasons for problems in teacher/learner situations:

## THE TEACHER:

Objectives Not Set: None were set, so none were met.

Improper Audience Analysis: The teacher did not relate to the students at the proper cultural, educational, or spiritual level.

Lack Of Proper Preparation: Insufficient time was given to lesson development.

Lack Of Prayer: Insufficient prayer time for students and the lesson.

Improper Methods: The methods were not suitable for the lesson taught, the age group or the culture. The methods did not keep the attention of the audience.

Discipline: Proper discipline was not maintained and students could not concentrate on the lesson.

Improper Presentation: The teacher talked too fast, too slow, not loud enough to be heard or there were communication barriers.

## THE STUDENT:

Unbelief: Jesus could not effectively minister in His own city because of unbelief of the audience (Matthew 13:58).

The Seed Of The Word Of God Did Not Fall On Good Ground: Read the parable of the sower in Matthew 13:1-9,18-23. Satan snatched the Word away, it withered when trials came, or the cares of the world caused it to die.

Inattention: The student did not pay attention because of distractions or discipline problems. They allowed Satan to snatch the Word from the good soil of their hearts (Matthew 13:19).

Refusal To Respond:   The student did not  become  a doer of the Word.  He heard the Word and did not reject the Word itself but refused to put it into practice in his life (Review James 1:22-25).  This was the problem of the rich young ruler who refused the Lord's call to discipleship (Mark 10:17-22).

Rejection Of The Message:   The  student  rejected  the message.  This was the problem when some disciples of Jesus turned back from following Him (John 6:53-66).

## USING PROBLEMS

Do not be discouraged by problems in the teaching situation.  Use them as opportunities to learn and improve your teaching tactics.  Problems can be corrected through prayer and change.  The teacher can change to correct some problems.  Students can change to correct others.

Jesus did not give up on His disciples.  He did not become discouraged by their faults and failures.  He saw them as what they could become when they allowed the Holy Spirit to work in their lives.  In the end, they proved worthy of this confidence.  In the book of Acts we find these doubting, fearful, denying men emerging as the great leaders of the first Church.

You can view problems as either opportunities or obstacles.  If you consider problems as obstacles, you will become discouraged and quit.  If you consider them as opportunities, you will grow spiritually and improve your skills in Biblical teaching.

# SELF-TEST

1. Write the Key Verse from memory.

_____

_____

2. Define "evaluation."

_____

3. Why is it important to evaluate your teaching?

_____

4. List four methods of evaluating Biblical teaching.

_____

_____

_____

_____

5. Summarize the common reasons for problems in the teacher/ learner situation.

_____

_____

6. How can you use problems in a positive way?

_____

_____

(Answers to self-tests are provided at the conclusion of the final chapter in this manual.)

# FOR FURTHER STUDY

## EVALUATING YOUR TEACHING

Evaluate yourself as a teacher.  Read each question and circle the number which you feel is most accurate.  Add up the total of the circled numbers.  A score of 85 and above would be an excellent score and 40 and below would be a poor score.  In between would range from fair (41-60) to good (61-84).Numbers indicate: 1=never 2=rarely 3=sometimes 4=often 5=always

### PREPARATION:

| | |
|---|---|
| I begin lesson preparation more than one week in advance. | 5 4 3 2 1 |
| The Bible is the center of my lesson preparation. | 5 4 3 2 1 |
| I have a systematic plan of lesson study. | 5 4 3 2 1 |
| I keep in mind the specific needs of my pupils as I prepare. | 5 4 3 2 1 |
| I write down a specific objective for each lesson. | 5 4 3 2 1 |
| I write out a lesson plan. | 5 4 3 2 1 |
| I pray regularly about my task. | 5 4 3 2 1 |
| I seek constantly to improve my teaching by reading, attending workers meetings or taking training courses. | 5 4 3 2 1 |

### PRESENTATION:

| | |
|---|---|
| I gain the interest of students from the beginning. | 5 4 3 2 1 |
| I have the Bible passages read meaningfully. | 5 4 3 2 1 |
| I conclude with a call for response. | 5 4 3 2 1 |
| I use a variety of teaching methods. | 5 4 3 2 1 |
| I am able to follow the subject to a conclusion without being diverted. | 5 4 3 2 1 |
| I give proper emphasis to the central truth. | 5 4 3 2 1 |
| I apply to life and ministry what is taught. | 5 4 3 2 1 |

### RESPONSE:

| | |
|---|---|
| My pupils are stimulated to more Bible study. | 5 4 3 2 1 |
| My teaching helps change lives. | 5 4 3 2 1 |
| My teaching reaches the lost for Christ. [evangelism]. | 5 4 3 2 1 |
| My teaching makes pupils faithful in church relationships. | 5 4 3 2 1 |
| My teaching helps promote spiritual maturity. | 5 4 3 2 1 |

# CHAPTER TWELVE

## CURRICULUM SELECTION AND DEVELOPMENT

**OBJECTIVES:**

Upon completion of this chapter you will be able to:

- Define "Biblical curriculum."
- Explain the value of Biblical curriculum.
- Select appropriate curriculum.
- Develop your own Biblical curriculum.

**KEY VERSES:**

> **All scripture is given <u>by inspiration</u> of God, and <u>is profitable</u> for doctrine, for reproof, for correction, for instruction in righteousness:**
>
> **That the man of God may be perfect, thoroughly furnished unto all good works. (II Timothy 3:16-17)**

## INTRODUCTION

The Bible is the basis for all instruction in the church. But Christian writers have developed some excellent materials that can assist in organizing training for one group or several groups of students. This lesson concerns the selection of Biblical curriculum.

## BIBLICAL CURRICULUM

The word "curriculum" refers to an organized course of study. It can refer to one course or all the courses used in a school. "Biblical curriculum" is an organized course of study of Biblical subject matter.

## THE VALUE OF BIBLICAL CURRICULUM

Biblical curriculum is a valuable tool in Christian teaching. Here are some reasons:

-It provides more research and background material than you may have access to or have time to prepare.

-It provides written lessons and activities for students.

-It provides an outline for teaching a lesson.

-It provides suggestions for how to teach the lesson.

-Some curriculum provides written objectives for each lesson.

-Most curriculum is prepared for specific age levels. It is written by people who are trained in working with that particular age group.

-An organized curriculum program provides wider coverage of Biblical truths. Most teachers tend to focus on certain portions of the Bible which they enjoy or feel comfortable teaching. Organized programs of curriculum cover the entire Bible over a period of time.

-It provides a way to organize teaching for many age groups in a local church.

## CURRICULUM SELECTION

The most important thing to remember in curriculum selection is that curriculum written by man is not our final authority. The Bible is the one and only authority for the Christian teacher. Curriculum must be carefully examined to be sure it is doctrinally sound.

Here is how to obtain and select curriculum:

1. In the "For Further Study" section of this chapter there is a list of curriculum publishers in the United States. If they do not publish materials in your language they can guide you to publishers who do. Write to several publishers and request information about their curriculum programs. Ask for sample materials. If your local church is part of an organized denomination, they may publish their own curriculum. Write to your denominational headquarters to obtain samples. Remember to consider Harvestime International Institute materials for your training program for adults.

2. While you are waiting for the materials to arrive, write general objectives for your total teaching program. (Use the skills you learned in Chapter Nine of this course). What are your general spiritual objectives for the groups for which you are obtaining materials? You will need to know these objectives in order to evaluate the curriculum to see if it meets these spiritual purposes.

3. When you receive the sample materials, use the checklist in this chapter to evaluate the material. If others will be teaching this curriculum, have them assist you in reviewing the

sample materials.

4. After you select the curriculum you want to use, prepare and mail the order. Use the order form the publisher will enclose with the sample package. Be sure to include the correct payment for the materials. Keep a <u>copy</u> of your order so you can verify that you receive what you ordered.

5. When the order arrives, immediately open the materials to make sure they have sent exactly what you ordered. Compare your copy of the original order to what they actually sent. If there are errors made in filling your order, notify the publisher immediately.

6. You may need to train others in how to use the curriculum. Chapter Fourteen in this course, *"Teacher Training,"* will assist you in doing this.

7. Store the material in a safe place until you are ready to use it.

## DEVELOP BIBLICAL CURRICULUM

If you do not have funds to purchase curriculum, develop it yourself. In Chapter Ten of this course you learned how to plan a Biblical lesson. Use these skills to develop a series of such lessons. Write these lessons out in detail. Eventually, you will have developed your own training course. Take the series of lessons you have written and evaluate them using the evaluation chart in this chapter. The chart will help you identify ways to improve the materials you have prepared.

It is slower to develop Biblical curriculum than to purchase it, but there are some advantages:

-You can design it specifically for the audience or culture for which you intend to use it.
-You can be certain of its doctrinal content.
-You can prepare it to meet specific spiritual objectives.

## CURRICULUM EVALUATION CHECKLIST

Use this evaluation checklist when reviewing curriculum materials:

## TEACHER'S MATERIALS:

### Objectives:

-What are the stated objectives?
-Are they similar to the objectives you have set for teaching/learning?
-Are they specific enough so that you can know when you have accomplished them?

## Content:

-Is the content doctrinally sound?
-Is it appropriate for your culture?
-Is the Biblical content appropriate for the learners at the age at which they will be using it?
-Is the interpretation of the Biblical material appropriate for the age at which it will be used? (Not too simple for older learners or too difficult for younger learners).
-Does the material help learners understand what it means to be part of the Christian community, its worship, structure, beliefs, history, mission?
-Does content support your church program?

## Life Experience:

-How does the material interpret the meaning of the Christian life? To what extent is this in agreement with your objectives?
-How does the material relate Christian living to Biblical learning?
-Does the material give opportunities to practice and reflect upon actions that express a Christian lifestyle?
-How does the material relate Christianity to living in family, school, community, world, and environment?

## Format:

-Is the format of the book attractive?
-Is each session clearly outlined so that a teacher can easily understand the steps for teaching?
-Are there particular features that help the teacher grasp the outline?
-What methods for teaching are suggested? With which of these are the teachers comfortable? Which new ones could be easily learned?
-Are instructions for activities clear and easy to follow?
-What resources are suggested for use beyond those in the book? Which of these are essential? Which could be easily obtained?
-Does the teacher's book include helpful material about the age and learning levels of those in the class?
-Is there background material about the lesson content so that teachers' information will be enriched?

## STUDENT'S MATERIALS:

## Reading Book:

-Is it attractively illustrated [from a child's viewpoint]?
-Is the print easy to read for a child?
-Would the style and language attract a child's interest?

-Is the story within a child's understanding?

## Workbook:

-Would the exercises be interesting to children?
-Are they too difficult?  Too easy?
-Would they enrich the understanding of the lesson?  How?
-Would they be helpful enough for the cost involved?   Or would it be better to develop
 activities specifically for the class?

## Activity Packet:

-Which activities are most likely to be used?  How often?
-Critically speaking, what is the quality of each item: poster, picture, etc.?
-Will children find the suggested activities useful, or could similar activities be constructed
 with little effort and less expense?

## Take-home Paper:

-What is the purpose of this paper as evidenced by its design and content?
-Would it reinforce the lesson for use at home?
-Would it enrich the material used in class?
-Would it be a link between absentees and the class?
-How valuable would it be as a contact with the families of children present in class?  Of those
 who were absent?
-Is it worth the price?  Why or why not?

## GENERAL PLAN OF CURRICULUM:

-What are the goals over a six, eight, or twelve-year span?

-List the basic content of each unit of the twelve-year span.

-Note the "flow" of the material:

> -How is Biblical material used: chronologically? topically? other?
> -What are the advantages/disadvantages of this design?
> -Where do repetitions of material occur?
> -Do these reinforce learning? deepen insights? fill space?
> -Are units planned for seasonal emphasis?  Are these useful?

-Is the cost within the budget of your congregation?  Is the program within the teaching skills
of your teachers?

-Is there space for additions or substitutions for special studies without disrupting the pattern [such as missions project, worship, stewardship]?

# SELF-TEST

1. Write the Key Verses from memory.

_____

_____

_____

_____

2. Define "Biblical curriculum."

_____

_____

_____

3. What is the value of Biblical curriculum?

_____

_____

4. How can you develop your own curriculum?

_____

_____

_____

(Answers to self-tests are provided at the conclusion of the final chapter in this manual.)

# FOR FURTHER STUDY

1. Most Biblical curriculum publishers follow a plan in their literature. Study the following information on how modern curriculum is planned:

## MODERN CURRICULUM PLANS

Here are the four basic plans evangelical publishers follow in grading their lesson materials. To evaluate curriculum, you need to study the advantages and disadvantages of each curriculum plan in terms of your own needs and objectives:

### UNIFORM GRADING:

How The Curriculum Is Organized:

The same Bible portion is taught to each age-group.

Advantages:

1. A small church can unite all pupils in a single lesson-related worship service.
2. All family members can discuss their common lesson at home.

Disadvantages:

1. Lessons are repeated on a 5-7 year cycle, provide limited Bible coverage.
2. Bible content often not suitable for pupils of all ages.

### UNIFIED GRADING:

How The Curriculum Is Organized:

Different Bible content, related by a single theme, is taught to each age-group.

Advantages:

1. Several age-groups can meet in a single theme-related worship service.
2. At-home discussion of the theme is possible.

Disadvantages:

1. Limited number of themes make it difficult to give complete Bible coverage.
2. Lessons taught in each department determined by theme, rather than pupils' needs.

## DEPARTMENT GRADING:

How The Curriculum Is Organized:

Different Bible content is provided for each age group.

Advantages:

1. All activities are closely related to the Bible lesson in each group.
2. Lessons can be geared to the social, psychological, emotional and mental level of all pupils.

Disadvantages:

1. Common at-home discussion is limited, since parents and children study different material.

## CLOSE GRADING:

How The Curriculum Is Organized:

Different Bible content is provided for pupils of each age.

Advantages:

1. Curriculum can be planned to fit the stage of development of pupils.

Disadvantages:

1. At-home discussion limited.
2. Hard to relate all activities to a common theme, since each age has a different lesson.

2. Use the following list to write and request samples of Biblical curriculum. All addresses are in the U.S.A.:

American Bible Society
450 Park Ave.
New York, N.Y. 10022

Assemblies of God
434 W. Pacific
Springfield, Mo. 65801

Christian Booksellers Association
5611 W. Chicago Ave.
Chicago, Ill. 60651

Warner Press (Church of God)
1303 E. 5th St.
Anderson, Ind.

Committee on Religious Education for the Mentally Retarded
210 N. Broadway
St. Louis, Mo. 63102

Concordia Publishing House
(Missouri Synod Lutheran)
3558 S. Jefferson Ave.
St. Louis, Mo. 63118

David C. Cook Publishing Co.
850 N. Grove
Elgin, Ill.

Evangelical Missions Information Service
1405 G St., N.W.
Washington, D.C. 20005

Evangelical Teacher Training Assn.
499 Gunderson
Wheaton, Ill. 60188

Gospel Light Publications
725 E. Colorado Blvd.
Glendale, Ca. 91205

Gospel Publishing House
1445 Boonville Ave.
Springfield, Mo. 65802

Greater Chicago Sunday School Assn.
5200 W. Washington Blvd.
Chicago, Ill. 60644

Moody Press
820 N. LaSalle St.
Chicago, Ill. 60610

National Association of Directors of Christian Education
175 N. Franklin St.
Chicago, Ill. 60606

National Sunday School Assn.
175 N. Franklin St.
Chicago, Ill. 60606

Scripture Press
1825 College Ave.
Wheaton, Ill. 60188

Southern Baptist Convention
127 9th Ave., No.
Nashville, Tenn. 37203

Standard Publishing
8100 Hamilton Ave.
Cincinnati, Ohio 45231

Zondervan Publishing House
1415 Lake Dr., S.E.
Grand Rapids, Mich. 49506

# CHAPTER THIRTEEN

## TEACHING ILLITERATE STUDENTS

**OBJECTIVES:**

Upon completion of this chapter you will be able to:

- Identify illiterate students.
- Summarize guidelines for teaching illiterate students.

**KEY VERSE:**

> **The fear of the Lord is the beginning of wisdom: and the knowledge of the holy is understanding. (Proverbs 9:10)**

### INTRODUCTION

Some teachers face the challenge of teaching illiterate students. An illiterate student is one who does not read or write his language. If you plan to teach illiterate students, you need to study this lesson. If you do not plan to teach illiterate students, you may skip this lesson and go on to Chapter Fourteen.

### CAN THEY BE TAUGHT?

A person does not have to know how to read and write in order to learn. For example, language is a difficult skill to acquire, yet children learn to speak their native language without knowing how to read and write. It is possible to teach illiterate students the truths of God's Word even though they cannot read it for themselves.

One of God's first commands to pass on His Word was to do it verbally:

> **And these words, which I command thee this day, shall be in thine heart;**

> **And thou shalt teach them diligently unto thy children, and shalt talk of them when thou sittest in thine house and when thou walkest by the way, and when thou liest down, and when thou risest up. (Deuteronomy 6:6-7)**

Jesus taught without using written material. He never handed out written lessons or had His students read passages from the Bible.

We can assume that Jesus taught people who were illiterate because His audiences included the poor who did not have access to education. These people did not read or write lessons Jesus taught. They relied on oral communication to learn.

If you are to teach the Gospel to every person, then you must have a plan to reach the illiterate. You cannot reach everyone with the written message of God's Word and you cannot assume they must learn to read before they can be reached with the Gospel.

Learning about God is not dependent upon education as much as it is heart attitude:

> **The fear of the Lord is the beginning of wisdom: and the knowledge of the holy is understanding. (Proverbs 9:10)**

## TEACHING ILLITERATE STUDENTS

Here are some guidelines for teaching illiterate students:

## WORK THROUGH CULTURAL LEADERS:

Illiterate people listen to and obey their leaders. If you can get the leaders to accept the message, it will be more easily communicated to the people. Once the leaders have accepted the message, they can communicate it easily to others because they are used to communicating without written materials.

## RELATE THE MESSAGE TO THE CULTURE:

You have learned that a message must be related to the listener to gain attention, make application, and achieve the proper response. Study the culture of the illiterate person. What are the concerns of their everyday life? What are the problems and challenges they face in their culture? Your message must be related to these concerns to gain attention, make proper application, and achieve response from the people.

## RELATE TEACHING METHODS TO THE CULTURE:

Most cultures have a traditional method of passing information from person to person. Some cultures do it through story telling. Others do it through songs and music that communicate their message. Study the culture to see how messages are best communicated. Identify methods commonly used in their culture and use them to teach Biblical truths.

## USE THE ENVIRONMENT:

Use the environment of the illiterate person. Select simple objects from their own culture to use as teaching aids. Remember how Jesus used stones, flowers, seed, birds, fish, candles, and buildings? You may need to create modern parables to illustrate truths. Jesus used parables that focused on fishing, planting and harvesting, etc., because His audience understood these things. Your audience may not understand these illustrations. Study the environment of the illiterate person you are teaching. Use their environment to create modern parables which illustrate Biblical truths.

## REPEAT SIMPLE PRINCIPLES:

Keep the lessons simple. Present simple, basic principles. Repeat these basic points several times to make sure the students have understood them. Have the students repeat the basic truths orally themselves.

## SUMMARIZE:

Present a brief statement at the conclusion of the lesson which summarizes the main truth you have been teaching. For example, in teaching the born-again experience of John 3 you could state at the conclusion: "You must be born again. It is a spiritual birth, not a physical one. You are born again spiritually by repenting of your sin and accepting Jesus as your Savior."

## ASK QUESTIONS:

When you are finished teaching a lesson, ask questions to be sure the basic principles of the lesson have been understood.

## CALL FOR RESPONSE:

One way to be sure the students have understood the message is to call for a response. For example, at the conclusion of a lesson on John 3, ask "How many of you would like to experience this new birth?"

## THE BIBLE: GOD'S BOOK

The Bible is a written message which God directed men to write. It is a book that contains His Words. His desire is for all men to be able to read it. For this reason, many Christian leaders have become involved in literacy training. This is a program which teaches illiterate people how to read and write so they will be able to read God's message for themselves. If you are interested in doing this, see the "For Further Study" section of this chapter. But remember, it is not necessary for a person to be able to read and write to respond to the Gospel.

# SELF-TEST

1. Write the Key Verse from memory.

_____

_____

_____

_____

2. Define the term "illiterate."

_____

_____

3. Summarize guidelines given in this lesson for teaching illiterate students.

_____

_____

_____

_____

(Answers to self-tests are provided at the conclusion of the final chapter in this manual.)

# FOR FURTHER STUDY

1. Find someone who is illiterate and share the Gospel with them using the guidelines given in this chapter.

2. If you are interested in starting a literacy program to help people learn to read and write in their own language, write to the following address for information:

Laubauch Literacy
Box 13
Syracuse, N.Y. 13210
U.S.A.

# CHAPTER FOURTEEN

## TEACHER TRAINING

**OBJECTIVES:**

Upon completion of this chapter you will be able to:

- Identify two basic needs for teacher training.
- Summarize steps for planning a teacher training program.
- Explain how to recruit students for a teacher training program.
- Summarize guidelines for conducting teacher training sessions.
- Summarize guidelines for placing trained teachers in the church.
- List ways a teacher may be evaluated.

**KEY VERSE:**

> **For I have given unto them the words which thou gavest me; and they have received them, and have known surely that I came out from thee, and they have believed that thou didst send me. (John 17:8)**

## INTRODUCTION

Jesus trained the disciples and upon conclusion of the training said...

> **For I have given unto them the words which thou gavest Me...**
> **(John 17:8)**

The Biblical plan of spiritual multiplication is teaching faithful men who are able to teach others also (II Timothy 2:2). If you are to fulfill this plan, you must constantly be training teachers. This lesson concerns the subject of teacher training. In this chapter, two basic needs for teacher training are discussed and practical steps are given for planning a training program. Guidelines are also given on how to recruit students for the training, how to conduct the sessions, and for placing trained teachers in the church.

## TWO BASIC TRAINING NEEDS

There are two basic needs for teacher training in the church: pre-service and in-service training.

## PRE-SERVICE TRAINING:

Pre-service training is training given <u>before</u> a believer begins to serve in the church as a teacher. It is a program of study that will help him learn how to teach.

## IN-SERVICE TRAINING:

In-service training is given to those <u>already serving</u> as teachers in the church. The training helps them further develop their teaching gift. Jesus provided both types of training for His disciples.

## PLANNING A TEACHER TRAINING PROGRAM

Here are steps for planning a teacher training program in your church:

1. Enlist the cooperation of the pastor or spiritual leader of the church.

2. Ask people who are already effective teachers to assist as leaders who will teach others.

3. Meet with these leaders to set:

-Objectives for the training program: Determine the needs of current teachers and potential teachers. State the objectives you want to accomplish in the training program.

-Dates, times, and place for training.

-Leaders who will teach in the training program: Who will teach what and when?

-Entrance requirements for the program: Who will you permit to attend? They must be born-again believers, of course, but you may have other requirements you want to set. (See suggestions in the "For Further Study" section of this chapter).

-Standards required for completion of the program: What is required of them to complete the training? (For suggestions, see the "For Further Study" section of this lesson).

-Type of training event: See the "For Further Study" section of this lesson for various types of training events.

-Budget [expenses] for teacher training: How much will it cost? Where will the funds come from?

-Training materials to be used: This course can be used to train teachers. You may want to supplement it with training unique to your denomination and/or the curriculum you plan to use.

4.  Prepare a calendar for the year and list all training sessions on it.  Include the dates, times, and places.

5.  Prepare a ministry description for teachers.  This will identify the responsibilities of a teacher for those who are considering enlisting in the training.  (See the "For Further Study" section of this lesson for a sample ministry description).

6.  Prepare a teacher's pledge for potential teachers to sign.  This is a document that identifies the commitment of the teacher.  (See the "For Further Study" section of this lesson for a sample pledge).

## RECRUITING FOR THE TRAINING PROGRAM

Here are steps for recruiting people for the teacher training program:

1.  Invite current teachers for in-service training.

2.  Make an announcement in church services regarding the training. Ask potential teachers who are interested to contact you.

3.  Make personal contact with those you know or have observed and whom you believe have the spiritual gift of teaching.

4.  Review applicants who are not already teaching to be certain they meet the entrance requirements you have set for the teacher training program.

5.  Notify all who qualify of the date, time and place of the first session.

## CONDUCTING THE TRAINING

Here are some guidelines for conducting teacher training sessions:

1.  Start each session on time.

2.  Begin with prayer that the Holy Spirit will anoint the teachers and will open the hearts and minds of students to learn.

3.  Take attendance.  Students should be required to attend a certain number of class sessions in order to complete the course.

4.  Make sure each student has a copy of any written materials concerning the lesson to be taught.

5. Have all necessary supplies on hand to teach the lesson. These might include visual aids, a teaching manual, and similar items. Use teaching methods you have learned in this course.

6. Allow time for questions and answers about the material you have taught in the session.

7. Give assignments for students to complete prior to the next meeting. These might include reading, writing, or teaching assignments.

8. Unless the Holy Spirit moves differently, keep within the time set for the class. Dismiss students on time.

## PLACING TEACHERS

Teacher training is not effective unless those you train are actually used in a teaching position. Here are some guidelines for placing teachers in the church educational program:

### CONSULT THE PASTOR:

Where does he have need for teachers? Where does he believe an individual would be most effective? The Pastor is the leader God has set in the church. He is responsible for the teaching program in the church. He is also responsible for guiding the gifts and talents of those who are part of the church.

### PLACE ACCORDING TO CALL AND ABILITIES:

Consider the abilities of the person being placed. Will they be effective in the group they are to teach? Has God given them a special call to this particular group? For example, the Apostle Paul was effective with Gentile people because of the call God gave Him and his personal background and abilities.

### PLACE ACCORDING TO AGE INTEREST:

Some people have no interest in teaching children. Others are not at ease with adults. All ages need to be taught, but a teacher should have either an interest and/or a call to work with a specific age group.

### ALLOW OPPORTUNITIES FOR PRACTICE TEACHING:

Let the new teacher serve first as a substitute teacher when the regular teacher cannot be present. Then let them teach several lessons with an experienced teacher observing. After the lesson, the observer can privately share helpful suggestions with the new teacher.

## TEACHER EVALUATION

After a teacher is serving in the church, their ministry should be evaluated periodically. Jesus did this with His disciples after He sent them out to minister. They reported back all they had said and done (Mark 6:7 and 30). Evaluation helps identify and correct problems in teaching. It gives an opportunity for spiritual leaders of the church to assist teachers in further developing their spiritual gift of teaching.

Here are some ways to evaluate a teacher:

1. The teacher may be evaluated using the evaluation skills learned in Chapter Eleven of this course. Have each teacher do a self-evaluation, then review the results with them.

2. Evaluate on the basis of the ministry description: Are they fulfilling the requirements of the ministry description for their teaching position?

3. Are they keeping the commitment of the teacher's pledge which they signed?

4. Observe the teacher actually teaching a lesson. Are they effectively communicating God's Word to their students? What can they do to improve the way they present the lesson? Share some positive suggestions with them.

5. Evaluate the fruit. The Bible says that "fruit" [results of ministry] can be observed (Luke 6:43-44).

Remember: Evaluation and correction of problems should always be done in a loving and positive way.

# SELF-TEST

1. Write the Key Verse from memory.

_____

_____

2. What are the two basic needs for teacher training?

_____

3. Summarize steps for planning a teacher training program.

_____

4. How can you recruit students for the teacher training program?

_____

5. Summarize guidelines for conducting teacher training sessions.

_____

_____

6. Summarize guidelines for placing trained teachers in the church.

_____

_____

7. List five ways to evaluate a teacher.

_____     _____

_____     _____

_____

(Answers to self-tests are provided at the conclusion of the final chapter in this manual.)

# FOR FURTHER STUDY

The following guide summarizes what you learned in this lesson.  You can use it to plan a teacher training program:

1.  List the objectives of your training program:

_____

_____

_____

_____

2.  Schedule the dates, times, and places on a master calendar for the year.  (Use a calendar to do this).

3.  Establish **entrance requirements** for the program. An applicant should:

-Be a born-again believer.
-Have followed the example of Christ in water baptism.
-Be Spirit-filled.
-Attend church services regularly (and/or be a member of the church).
-Have a good reputation in church and community.
-Meet Biblical qualifications for leaders.
-Demonstrate fruit of the Holy Spirit and Christ-like behavior in daily living.

4.  Set **standards for completion of program**. Here are some suggestions:

Applicants must:

-Attend all training sessions unless excused due to illness or emergency approved by class
 leader.
-Complete all class assignments.
-Practice teach at least one lesson with a leader observing.

5.  Determine the **type of teacher training event**.  Here are some suggestions:

-Brief training as part of regular teachers' meeting:  If the teachers of the church meet regularly, use part of each meeting for in-service training.

-During Sunday School hour: If your church has a Sunday School hour, train new teachers in a special class conducted during this time.

-Self-instruction: Give potential teachers a copy of this manual and have them complete the lessons in individual study.

-One-night training: Meet one night a week to train.

-Series: Meet in a series of meetings for training. For example, Monday through Friday of a certain week.

-Retreat: Take teachers to a camp or retreat for training.

-One-to-one: Assign an experienced teacher to train a new teacher on a one-to-one basis.

-United training: Perhaps several churches in the community may want to plan a united training event where all the teachers of their denomination come together for fellowship and training.

-Audio-visual training: If you have audio or video tape facilities, record the training and let students study independently.

6. Select **the leaders who will teach**, what areas they will cover, and when they will teach. Make a chart with the following headings:

<u>Name</u>             <u>Dates</u>                      <u>Subjects</u>

7. What training materials will you use?

Name of training course: _____

Publisher's Name/Address:_____

(Don't forget...You can use this manual by Harvestime to train teachers.)

8. Prepare a budget:

    What will it cost to advertise the program?    $_____

    What will the training materials cost?    $_____

    Other expenses:    $_____

9. Prepare a ministry description of responsibilities for potential teachers. Here is an example to follow:

SAMPLE MINISTRY DESCRIPTION

Adult Class Teacher

Ministry Title: Adult class teacher.

Ministry Description: The adult class Bible study teacher will assume personal responsibility for:

-Preparing for and teaching the weekly class session.

    Day_____Time_____Place_____

-Recruiting new members to join the class.

-Contacting absentee students and inactive members to determine problems, minister, and reinstate as active members.

-Winning unsaved members to the Lord Jesus Christ.

-Ministering to the spiritual needs of class members who are already believers, leading them in spiritual growth and development, equipping them for the work of the ministry.

-Encouraging class members to become an active part of the total church fellowship.

-Completing any required church records pertaining to this class ,i.e., attendance records, etc.

Personal Requirements:

-Called of God to this specific ministry.
-Meet Biblical leadership qualifications.

-Completion of teacher training course offered by this church.
-Ability to communicate effectively.
-Active member of this church fellowship.
-In agreement with the doctrinal position of this church.
-Supportive and in harmony with church leadership.

Time Commitment:

-Personal preparation time for regular class meeting.
-Regular class meeting time: Two hours weekly.
-Monthly staff meeting.
-Annual in-service teacher's training class.
-Time for personal association, fellowship, follow-up, and ministry to students.

10.  Prepare a **teacher's pledge of commitment**.  Here is an example to follow:

TEACHER'S COMMITMENT

Having received Jesus Christ as personal Savior, and now living in fellowship with Him,  I realize that ministering Christ and His word to others is a high calling.  In view of my commission as a teacher and relying on the help and guidance of the Holy Spirit,  I pledge that:

-I agree with the doctrinal statement of my church, and will teach nothing in conflict with it.
-I will daily set aside time for prayer and Bible study.
-I will earnestly pray for the conversion of my students and for the spiritual growth of those who are
 Christians.
-I will faithfully spend time preparing each lesson, and will prepare myself spiritually by living the truths I
 teach.
-I will be faithful in my teaching position in the church.
-I will teach in class from God's Word, promote study of the Bible by my students and encourage their active
 participation in class.
-I will faithfully attend and promote the services of our church, and will support the church financially and with
 my prayers.
-I will attend  any meetings of the church department, unless hindered by some reason I can conscientiously give
 to God.
-If for some reason I cannot fulfill my responsibilities, I will  consult with my leaders and surrender my class if
 that seems advisable.

Name:_____Date:_____

# CHAPTER FIFTEEN

## AN INTRODUCTION TO PREACHING

**OBJECTIVES:**

Upon completion of this chapter you will be able to:

- Define preaching.
- Identify subjects upon which Biblical preaching should focus.
- Explain the importance of demonstrating God's power when preaching the Word.
- Identify six Biblical warnings regarding preaching.

**KEY VERSES:**

> **How then shall they call on Him in whom they have not believed? and how shall they believe in Him of whom they have not heard? and how shall they hear without a preacher? And how shall they preach, except they be sent? (Romans 10:14-15a)**

## INTRODUCTION

This chapter introduces the subject of Biblical preaching. It defines preaching, identifies the subjects of Biblical preaching, explains the importance of the demonstration of God's power when preaching, and identifies Biblical warnings regarding preaching. In the next chapter you will learn how to plan a Biblical sermon.

## TEACHING AND PREACHING

You learned the definition of "teaching" in Chapter One of this course:

> Teaching is the act of instructing others. It includes showing, demonstrating, informing, imparting knowledge, training, and guiding the studies of another.

Here is the definition of "preaching":

> Preaching is the act of delivering a discourse [a sermon or systematic examination of a subject] which instructs others in a formal manner.

Preaching and teaching are similar, in that they both communicate the truths of God's Word to others. You will learn in the next chapter that preparing a sermon is similar to preparing a lesson to teach. But preaching and teaching usually differ in the methods of instruction used and the style of delivery.

## COMBINING PREACHING AND TEACHING

The effective sharing of the Gospel combines both preaching and teaching. Jesus taught and preached:

> **And Jesus went about all the cities and villages, teaching in their synagogues, and preaching the Gospel of the Kingdom, and healing every sickness and every disease among the people. (Matthew 9:35)**

(See also Matthew 4:17,23; 9:35; 11:1,5; Mark 1:14,38-39; 2:2; Luke 4:43-44; 9:6; 20:1; I Peter 3:19; 4:6).

One of the main missions of Jesus was to preach:

> **The Spirit of the Lord is upon me, because He hath anointed me to preach the Gospel to the poor...to preach deliverance to the captives...to preach the acceptable year of the Lord. (Luke 4:18-19)**

Jesus died in order that repentance and remission of sins could be preached:

> **And said unto them, Thus it is written, and thus it behooved Christ to suffer, and to rise from the dead the third day:**

> **And that repentance and remission of sins should be preached in His name among all nations, beginning at Jerusalem. (Luke 24:46-47)**

## THE COMMISSION TO PREACH

The disciples were commissioned by Jesus to preach:

> **And He ordained twelve, that they should be with Him, and that He might send them forth to preach. (Mark 3:14)**

> **And as ye go, preach, saying, The Kingdom of Heaven is at hand. (Matthew 10:7) (See also Matthew 10:27; Luke 9:2,60).**

The goal of the early church was to preach the Gospel to those who had not yet heard it:

To preach the Gospel in the regions beyond you, and not to boast in another man's line of things made ready to our hand.
(II Corinthians 10:16)

Like teaching, preaching was not confined just to the formal church setting:

And daily in the temple, and in every house, they ceased not to teach and preach Jesus Christ. (Acts 5:42)

Neither was preaching confined to just the full-time pastors or ministers. Believers in the first church were scattered because of persecution and...

...they that were scattered abroad went everywhere preaching the Word.
(Acts 8:4) (See also Acts 11:19-20).

As believers, we also are commissioned to preach the Gospel to the nations of the world:

And this Gospel of the Kingdom shall be preached in all the world for a witness unto all nations; and then shall the end come. (Matthew 24:14)

Go ye into all the world and preach the Gospel to every creature.
(Luke 16:15)

## THE SUBJECT OF PREACHING

Like teaching, preaching should always be based on God's Word. For example, in the sermon of Peter in Acts 2, 12 of the 23 verses were quotations from Old Testament Scripture.

Biblical preaching should focus on:

## REPENTANCE AND FORGIVENESS OF SINS:

And that repentance and remission of sins should be preached in His name among all nations, beginning at Jerusalem. (Luke 24:47)

And they went out, and preached that men should repent. (Mark 6:12)
(See also Acts 13:38; 14:15).

## THE GOSPEL OF THE KINGDOM OF GOD:

And this Gospel of the Kingdom shall be preached in all the world for a witness unto all nations, and then shall the end come. (Matthew 24:14)

(See also Matthew 9:35; 11:5; Mark 1:14; 16:15; Luke 4:18; Acts 8:12; 14:7,21; 16:10; 20:25; Romans 1:15; 15:19-20; I Corinthians 15:1; II Corinthians 2:12; 10:14; 11:7; Colossians 1:23; I Thessalonians 2:9).

## THE RESURRECTION OF THE DEAD:

...preached through Jesus the resurrection from the dead. (Acts 4:2) (See also Acts 17:3,18).

## THE WORD OF GOD:

And straightway many were gathered together, insomuch that there was no room to receive them, no not so much as about the door: And He preached the Word unto them. (Mark 2:2)

But the Word of the Lord endureth for ever. And this is the Word which by the Gospel is preached unto you. (I Peter 1:25)

(See also Acts 8:4,25; 13:5; 14:25; 15:35-36; 17:13; II Timothy 4:2; Titus 1:3).

## THE WORD OF FAITH:

...The Word is nigh thee, even in thy mouth, and in thy heart: that is, the word of faith, which we preach. (Romans 10:8) (See also Galatians 1:23).

## ALL THINGS CONCERNING JESUS:

...Preaching the Kingdom of God, and teaching those things which concern the Lord Jesus Christ...(Acts 28:31)

Unto me, who am less than the least of all saints, is this grace given, that I should preach among the Gentiles the unsearchable riches of Christ. (Ephesians 3:8)

(See also Acts 5:42; 8:5,35; 9:20; 17:3,18; Romans 16:25; II Corinthians 1:19; 4:5; Colossians 1:28).

## PEACE THROUGH JESUS CHRIST:

The Word which God sent unto the children of Israel, preaching peace by Jesus Christ... (Acts 10:36) (See also Ephesians 2:17).

## THE CROSS:

**For the preaching of the cross is to them that perish foolishness; but unto us which are saved it is the power of God. (I Corinthians 1:18) (See also I Corinthians 1:17-22).**

## THE DEMONSTRATION OF POWER

The demonstration of God's power is to accompany preaching as well as teaching:

**And Jesus went about all the cities and villages, teaching in their synagogues, and preaching the Gospel of the Kingdom, and healing every sickness and every disease among the people. (Matthew 9:35)**

Paul said:

**And my speech and my preaching was not with enticing words of man's wisdom, but in demonstration of the Spirit and of power;**

**That your faith should not stand in the wisdom of men, but in the power of God. (I Corinthians 2:4-5) (See Mark 1:39; Luke 9:6; Romans 15:19; I Corinthians 1:17-18).**

The demonstration of power is important because it confirms the preaching of the Word:

**And they went forth and preached everywhere, the Lord working with them, and confirming the Word with signs following. (Mark 16:20)**

## THE PREACHER

Earlier in this course we discussed personal qualities that should be evident in the life of a teacher. These same qualities should also be in the life of one who preaches the Gospel. Colossians chapter 1 identifies three additional qualities of a preacher of the Gospel:

## HE IS A MINISTER OF CHRIST:

"A faithful minister of Christ" (Verse 7). Christ must be exalted in all his preaching.

## HE IS A MINISTER OF THE GOSPEL:

"The Gospel...whereof I, Paul, am made a minister" (Verse 23).

## HE IS A MINISTER OF THE CHURCH:

"...The church, whereof I am made a minister" (Verses 24-25).

## BIBLICAL WARNINGS

Here are four Biblical warnings regarding preaching:

## PREACHERS MUST LIVE WHAT THEY PREACH:

> Thou therefore which teachest another, teachest thou not thyself? Thou that preachest a man should not steal, dost thou steal? (Romans 2:21)

> But I keep under my body, and bring it into subjection; lest that by any means, when I have preached to others, I myself should be a castaway. (I Corinthians 9:27)

## IF YOU ARE CALLED TO PREACH, IT IS NOT AN OPTION:

Preaching is not an option for those specifically called by God to do so:

> For though I preach the Gospel, I have nothing to glory of; for necessity is laid upon me; yea, woe is unto me, if I preach not the Gospel. (I Corinthians 9:16)

## PREACHING MUST BE BASED ON GOD'S WORD:

> But though we, or an angel from Heaven, preach any other Gospel unto you than that which we have preached unto you, let him be accursed.

> And we said before, so say I now again, if any may preach any other gospel unto you than that ye have received let him be accursed. (Galatians 1:8-9) (See also II Corinthians 11:4).

## MOTIVES MUST BE RIGHT:

Paul discusses motives for preaching the Gospel in Philippians 1:15-18. Read this passage in your Bible. Paul noted that...

> Some indeed preach Christ even of envy and strife; and some also of good will. (Philippians 1:15)

# SELF-TEST

1. Write the Key Verses from memory.

_____

_____

2. Define "preaching."

_____

_____

3. On what subjects should Biblical preaching focus?

_____

_____

4. List four Biblical warnings regarding preaching which were discussed in this lesson.

_____

_____

_____

_____

5. Why is the demonstration of God's power important when preaching the Word?

_____

_____

(Answers to self-tests are provided at the conclusion of the final chapter in this manual.)

# FOR FURTHER STUDY

Study these Biblical references on preaching:

## OLD TESTAMENT REFERENCES ON PREACHING

Psalms 40:9; Ecclesiastes 1:1,2,12; 7:27; 11:8-10; Isaiah 61:1; Nehemiah 6:7.

## NEW TESTAMENT REFERENCES TO OLD TESTAMENT PREACHERS

Matthew 12:41;  Luke 11:32;  II Peter 2:5

## NEW TESTAMENT REFERENCES ON PREACHING

Matthew 3:1, 4:17,23; 9:35; 10:7,27; 11:1,5; 12:41; 24:14,41; 26:13

Mark 1:4,7,14,38-39;  2:2;  3:14;  6:12; 14:9; 16:15,20;

Luke 3:3,18;  4:18-19,43-44

Acts 3:20; 4:2; 5:42; 8:4,5,12,25,35,40; 9:20,27; 10:36-37,42; 11:19-20; 13:5,24,38,42; 14:7,15,21,25; 15:21,35-36; 16:6,10; 17:3,13,18; 19:13; 20:7,9,25

Romans 1:15; 2:21; 10:8-15; 15:19-20; 16:25

I Corinthians 1:17-18; 2:4; 9:14-16,18,27; 15:1-2,11,12,14

II Corinthians 1:19; 2:12; 4:5; 10:14; 10:16; 11:4,7

Galatians 1:8,9,11,16,23; 2:2; 3:8; 4:13; 5:11

Ephesians 2:17; 3:8;    Philippians 1:15-18;    Colossians 1:23,28; I Thessalonians 2:9;  I Timothy 2:7; 3:16; II Timothy 1:11; 4:17; Titus 1:3; Hebrews 4:2,6; I Peter 1:12,25; 3:19; 4:6; II Peter 2:5

# CHAPTER SIXTEEN

## PLANNING A SERMON

**OBJECTIVES:**

Upon completion of this chapter you will be able to:

- Summarize basic steps for planning a sermon.
- Define topical preaching.
- Define textual preaching.
- Define expository preaching.
- Plan a sermon to preach.

**KEY VERSE:**

**Preach the word; be instant in season, out of season; reprove, rebuke, exhort with all longsuffering and doctrine. (II Timothy 4:2)**

## INTRODUCTION

In this lesson you will learn how to preach a Biblical sermon. You will learn basic principles of preaching by studying some of the sermons in the Bible and some of the most effective sermons of great preachers throughout church history. You will discover that preaching and teaching are similar in many ways but differ in methods of presentation and style of delivery.

## PREACHING AND TEACHING: HOW THEY DIFFER

Preaching and teaching usually differ in the following ways:

**THE METHODS:**

Methods which call for audience participation are not commonly used in preaching. For example, there is usually no discussion or question and answer period when you preach. The reason is that preaching usually involves a larger audience. Because of this, the method of presentation is more formal.

## THE STYLE OF DELIVERY:

In teaching, people are often divided by age groups. The class is all adults, young people, or children. Preaching usually involves a group of people of various ages. The audience is not divided by age groups as they often are in Sunday school or church study groups.

For this reason, you must adjust your preaching style to a common level. Do not make the sermon so difficult that children and teenagers cannot understand. At the same time, do not make it so simple that adults lose interest.

## CURRICULUM:

Sunday schools and church schools often have curriculum guides which give you the subject and a discussion of the lesson you will teach. This is usually not true for preaching. With the direction of the Lord, you must determine the type and content of your message.

## PREPARING A SERMON

The basic steps in preparing a sermon are similar to those you learned in planning a lesson to teach. You should:

-Prepare yourself spiritually.
-Analyze the audience.
-Set objectives.

The basic structure of a sermon follows that of teaching a lesson. Your sermon should include:

-A title.
-The introduction.
-The body.
-The application.
-The conclusion.
(Review Chapter Ten, "Lesson Planning").

Just as you do in teaching, you must gain and hold the attention of the audience. You must present the lesson in an orderly way. You must make life and ministry applications in the sermon and you must call for response to the revelation of God's Word.

## TYPES OF SERMONS

From the study of Biblical sermons and the sermons of great preachers throughout Church history, three basic types of sermons have been identified:

## TYPE ONE - TOPICAL SERMONS:

Topical sermons focus on specific topics such as spiritual fruit, spiritual warfare, spiritual gifts, etc.

### How To Plan A Topical Sermon:

1. Determine the general topic of the sermon. For example, "prayer" may be the topic you select.

2. Determine the specific theme: On what theme of prayer will you preach? Here are some possibilities:

| | |
|---|---|
| -The Necessity of Prayer | -Intercessory Prayer |
| -The Value of Prayer | -Family Prayer |
| -The Times for Prayer | -Hindrances to Prayer |
| -The Power of Prayer | -Bible Prayers |
| -The Purpose of Prayer | -Practical Prayer |
| -The Method of Prayer | -Attitudes in Prayer |
| -The Results of Prayer | -Places to Pray |
| -The Conditions of Prayer | -Worship through Prayer |
| -The Problems of Prayer | -Posture in Prayer |
| -Praying in the Spirit | -The Privilege of Prayer |
| -Perseverance in Prayer | -Faith and Prayer |
| -The Preeminence of Prayer | -The Scope of Prayer |
| -Answers to Prayer | |

You must determine a specific theme for your sermon. You cannot cover every aspect of a topic because, as you see in this example, there are many themes to most Biblical topics. The theme you select will become the title of your sermon. For example, you may choose to speak on "Hindrances To Prayer."

3. Research everything the Bible has to say on the theme you have selected. If you have access to Bible research materials such as concordances, commentaries, and word study books, use these in your study also.

4. Develop the outline following the simple four-section structure you learned in Chapter Ten on lesson planning:

-Introduction
-Body
-Application
-Conclusion

## An Example Of A Topical Sermon:

Using the example theme "Hindrances To Prayer," your rough outline might look like the following:

Title: HINDRANCES TO PRAYER

Introduction: Focus on problems most people have: Unanswered prayer and the question as to why prayers are unanswered. This will gain attention as most everyone has experienced this problem.

Body: Discuss the hindrances to prayer identified in God's Word:

-Wrong motives and requests: James 4:2-3
-Sin of any kind: Isaiah 59:1-2
-Idols in the heart: Ezekiel 14:1-3
-An unforgiving spirit: Mark 11:25
-Selfishness: Proverbs 21:13
-Wrong treatment of marriage partner: I Peter 3:7
-Self-righteousness: Luke 18:10-14
-Unbelief: James 1:6-7
-Not abiding in Christ and His Word: John 15:7

Application:

I. Explain how unanswered prayer hinders:

    A. Family life.
    B. Our personal spiritual development.
    C. Our ministry.

II. Ask the audience to apply these truths individually:

    A. Which hindrances are blocking my prayers?

Conclusion:

I. Summarize the hindrances of prayer discussed.

II. Call for confession and repentance of those things which have hindered prayer.

## TYPE TWO - TEXTUAL SERMONS:

In textual preaching, a key Biblical passage forms the central truth or text of the lesson. The remainder of the message is built on this one central truth.

### How To Plan A Textual Sermon:

1. Select the text.

2. Develop a sermon title from the text.

3. Study the text in detail. Then study other Scriptural passages that relate to the text you have selected. If you have access to Bible research materials such as concordances, commentaries, and word study books, use these to further research the text.

4. Develop the outline following the simple four-section structure you learned in Chapter Ten on lesson planning:

    -Introduction
    -Body
    -Application
    -Conclusion

### An Example Of A Textual Sermon:

Peter's sermon in Acts 2:14-36 is a good example of this. If Peter had a title for the sermon, it may have been...THIS IS THAT.

Introduction:  Peter opened the message with reference to a Scripture text:

> **But this is that which was spoken by the prophet Joel;**
>
> **And it shall come to pass in the last days, saith God, I will pour out of my Spirit upon all flesh; and your sons and your daughters shall prophesy, and your young men shall see visions, and your old men shall dream dreams:**
>
> **And on my servants and on my handmaidens I will pour out in those days of my Spirit and they shall prophesy...  (Acts 2:16-18)**

This introduction gained the attention of the audience because they were watching the fulfillment of this passage right before their eyes!

Body:  The body of Peter's sermon focused on the text.

I.   He presented the historical background of the passage which was that day being fulfilled.
II.  He showed how it related to Israel's history and to Jesus Christ.

Application:  He made personal application...

> **For the promise is unto you, and to your children, and to all that are afar
> off, even as many as the Lord our God shall call.  (Acts 2:39)**

Conclusion:  He called for response...

> **Then Peter said unto them, Repent, and be baptized every one of you in the
> name of Jesus Christ for the remission of sins, and ye shall receive the gift
> of the Holy Ghost.  (Acts 2:38)**

And the audience responded...

> **Then they that gladly received his word were baptized: and the same day
> there were added unto them about three thousand souls.  (Acts 2:41)**

## TYPE THREE - EXPOSITORY SERMONS:

"Expository" is the title given to a method of preaching which focuses on a Scriptural passage
and explains it in detail, verse by verse.  The word "expository" means "to take apart and
examine the parts of a whole."

Expository is a more detailed type of preaching than topical or textual.  It can focus on a
specific subject or passage of Scripture, explaining it in detail, verse by verse and word by
word.  It can also focus on a book of the Bible, studying the book in detail, chapter by chapter,
then verse by verse, and even discussing in depth the meaning of key words.   Expository
preaching can focus on a biography, studying verse by verse all that is recorded regarding a
selected Biblical character.

Because expository preaching is so detailed, it often results in a series of messages.  It is not
possible to discuss in detail everything about a Bible passage, book, or personality in one
sermon.  Each sermon in the series should relate to the others.  When you begin each sermon
you should show how it relates to those which have preceded it.  You can do this by briefly
summarizing the previous messages and explaining how they relate to the one you are
presenting.

Although each sermon in a series should relate to the others, each sermon should also be
complete in itself.  Everyone in the audience may not be present for every sermon in the
series.  They should be able to understand each sermon without having heard the others.

## How To Plan An Expository Sermon:

1. Select the text, subject, Bible character, or book on which you plan to focus your message or series of messages.

2. Study in detail everything the Bible teaches on the text, subject, Bible character or book. If you have access to Bible research materials such as concordances, commentaries, and word study books, use these for further research.

3. Determine if your subject can be covered in a single expository sermon or if it will require a series of sermons.

4. Develop a title and text for each message in the series.

5. Develop an outline for each message in the series. Follow the simple four-section structure for each message:

-Introduction
-Body
-Application
-Conclusion

## An Example Of An Expository Sermon:

Here is an example of an outline for an expository sermon:

Title: CHARACTERISTICS OF FALSE TEACHERS

Text: Jude chapter 1

Introduction: Jude 1:3-4

Body:

I. Their background:

    A. Before of old ordained to this condemnation (verse 4).

II. Their walk:

    A. Crept in unawares (verse 4).
    B. Walking after their own lusts (verse 6).

C. Walking after their own <u>ungodly</u> lusts (verse 18).

III. Their talk:

    A. Speak evil of dignities (verses 8-10).
    B. Speak evil of things they know not (verses 8-10).
    C. Murmurers (verse 16).
    D. Complainers (verse 16).
    E. Mouths speak great swelling words (verse 16).
    F. Mockers (verse 18).

IV. Their doctrine:

    A. Turn the grace of God into lasciviousness (verse 4).
    B. Deny the only Lord God and our Lord Jesus Christ (verse 4).
    C. Have not the Spirit (verse 19).

V. Their conduct:

    A. Ungodly (verse 4).
    B. Filthy dreamers (verse 8).
    C. Defile the flesh (verse 8).
    D. Despise dominion (verses 8-10).
    E. Corrupt what they naturally know (verses 8-10).
    F. Admire people because of the benefit they receive (verse 16).
    G. Separate themselves (verse 19).
    H. Live sensually (verse 19).

<u>Application</u>: What should you do in response to these types: Jude 1:20-23

<u>Conclusion</u>: Summary, call for response.

## **GENERAL GUIDELINES**

Here are some general guidelines that will help you plan any type of sermon.

## **SELECTING A TEXT:**

The word "text" came from a Greek word which means "woven or spun." The text should be that from which the message is woven or from which it "spins off." It should be the basis of the sermon.

Using a text from God's Word as the basis of a sermon gives the preacher authority in his message. He is saying "Thus saith the Lord" because he is speaking God's Word. He can do so with boldness and authority. The text keeps a message Biblical and it gains the confidence of the audience by assuring them that the preacher is proclaiming God's Word and not his own opinions.

Here are some guidelines for selecting a text from God's Word:

1. Pray for guidance from the Lord.

2. Study God's Word regularly. Texts and subjects for ministry will result from your study. Keep a notebook of texts and subject ideas as you discover them in your personal study. Use these later for planning sermons.

3. Consider the spiritual needs of the audience to which you plan to minister. For example, an audience of ministers do not normally need a sermon on salvation. (Remember what you learned about audience analysis in Chapter Eight).

4. Before you preach on a text, be certain you understand it so you will not create confusion in the minds of your listeners.

5. Consider the entire revelation of God's truth. Do not preach only on your favorite texts or subjects people enjoy hearing. "ALL" Scripture is given by inspiration of God and profitable.

## INTERPRETING THE TEXT:

After you have selected a text, study all the Bible teaches about it. If you have various translations of the Bible, study these for further understanding. If you have Bible commentaries, read what others have said about the text. These study methods will help you understand and interpret the text properly.

Here are some basic rules of interpreting God's Word which should be used as you study the text:

**The Rule Of Divine Authority**: The Bible is the final authority. Every portion of the Scripture is inspired by God.

**The Rule Of Literal Interpretation**: The Bible means exactly what it says and should be interpreted literally unless the context indicates otherwise. Sometimes there are symbols and parables used in the Bible to illustrate truths, but these are clearly indicated in the context of Scripture.

**The Rule Of Contextual Consideration**: Every verse should be studied in relation to its context. Study what precedes and follows the text. Many false doctrines have been created by taking verses out of context. To study a passage in its context ask yourself:

-Who is speaking or writing?
-What is being said?
-To whom is it being said?
-Why is it said?
-When was it said?

**The Rule Of First Mention:** The first time a word, phrase, object, or incident is mentioned in the Bible, it often gives a key to its meaning anywhere else in the Bible.

For example, in Genesis 3 there is the first mention of fig leaves. Here, Adam used fig leaves to try to cover his own sin and nakedness by his own efforts. Fig leaves speak of self-righteousness, rejection of God, and an attempt to justify ones self before God.

This is why Jesus cursed the tree with leaves but no fruit in Matthew 21 and Mark 11 and 13. To understand this act, we recall the law of first mention and go back to Genesis 3. Fig leaves represented the self-righteous nation of Israel who had rejected Jesus and not brought forth the true fruits of repentance.

**The Rule Of Repetition:** When something is repeated in Scripture it is for the purpose of emphasis. It means that this truth is of such special importance that it needs to be repeated.

**The Rule Of Cumulative Revelation:** The full truth of God's Word on any subject must not be gathered from an isolated passage. The cumulative [total] revelation of all the Bible says regarding a truth must be considered. This means you must accumulate all the Bible teaches on a certain subject. This is why the rule is called the rule of "cumulative" revelation. You cannot base a doctrine on a few isolated verses about a subject.

**GATHERING SERMON MATERIAL:**

Once you have selected a text, you must gather material for the sermon. Asking these questions will help you do this:

1. What does the Bible teach about this subject? The most important objective is to communicate what God has revealed in His Word concerning the subject. This should compose the major part of your message.

2. What have I observed in life and ministry that concerns this subject? What examples in life and ministry relate to the subject? How have you seen the truths of the Word demonstrated in real life? You can use these examples for illustration and application in the message.

3.  What have I read concerning this subject?  If you have access to Bible reference materials, read and research the works of Bible scholars to gather materials for the sermon.

4.  Who do I know that has knowledge on this subject?  Is there someone who has had an experience which relates to this text?  Is there someone you know who has studied extensively on the subject?  Consult them as part of your preparation for preaching on this subject.

## THE FINAL OBJECTIVE

This chapter concludes this course on *"Teaching Tactics."* But in reality, you have only begun because you must keep on preaching and teaching until the final objective is met:

> **Whom we preach, warning every man, and teaching every man in all wisdom; that we may present every man perfect in Christ Jesus. (Colossians 1:28)**
>
> **And they shall not teach every man his neighbor, and every man his brother, saying Know the Lord; for all shall know me, from the least to the greatest. (Hebrews 8:11)**

# SELF-TEST

1. Write the Key Verse from memory.

_____

_____

2. Explain the relationship between preaching and teaching. How are they alike? How do they differ?

_____

3. Summarize basic steps for planning a sermon.

_____

_____

_____

4. Define "topical preaching."

_____

_____

5. Define "textual preaching."

_____

_____

6. Define "expository preaching."

_____

_____

7. Summarize guidelines given for selecting a text.

_____

_____

_____

8. Summarize guidelines for interpreting the text.

_____

_____

_____

9. Summarize the suggestions given in this lesson for gathering sermon material.

_____

_____

_____

(Answers to self-tests are provided at the conclusion of the final chapter in this manual.)

# FOR FURTHER STUDY

1. Study the following great Biblical sermons:

   -Moses' Farewell Sermon:  Deuteronomy 29-33

   -Joshua's Farewell Sermon:  Joshua 24:2-15

   -Samuel Addresses Israel:  I Samuel 12

   -Solomon's Dedication Message:  I Kings 8:15-61

   -Jeremiah Addresses The People At A Feast:  Jeremiah 7

   -Examples Of Sermons Of Jesus: Matthew 5-7; 11:7-19; 12:25-37; 13; 15:10-20; 21:28-44; 24-25; John 3:3-21; 6:26-58; 14-16.

   -Sermons of Peter:  Acts 2:14-36; 3:12-26

   -Sermons of Paul:  Acts 13:16-41; 17:22-31; 20:17-35; 22:1-21; 26:2-23

   -Stephen's Final Sermon:  Acts 7:2-53

2. Use the form on the next page to analyze a sermon to which you listen.  Then use the form to evaluate your own preaching.

# SERMON-EVALUATION FORM

## ORGANIZATION

**INTRODUCTION:**

Does it get attention?_____Does it touch some need directly or indirectly?_____

Does it orient you to the subject or the main idea?_____

Is it the right length?_____ Is there a specific purpose?_____

**BODY:**

Is the development clear?_____ Is the overall structure clear?_____

Does the sermon have a central idea?_____ Can you state it?_____

Are the transitions clear?_____ Do they review?_____

Is there a logical link between the points?_____

Do the main points relate back to the main idea?_____

Are the subpoints clearly related to their main points?_____

**APPLICATION:**

Is this subject significant?_____ Is it appropriate?_____

Is the sermon built on proper Biblical interpretation?_____

Does the speaker show you where he is in the text?_____

Is the analysis of the subject thorough?_____

**CONCLUSION:**

Does the sermon build to a climax?_____Is there an adequate summary of ideas?_____

Are there effective closing appeals or suggestions for response?_____

## STYLE

Does the speaker use correct grammar?_____Are words pronounced correctly?_____

Is his vocabulary varied?_____ Are words used correctly?_____

Does the choice of words add to the effectiveness of the sermon?_____

## DELIVERY

### ORAL PRESENTATION:

Does the speaker want to be heard?_____ Do you feel he is talking with you?_____

Is he friendly?_____ Does the delivery sound like lively conversation?_____

Is the voice easy to listen to?_____ Is it clear?_____

Is there vocal variety?_____ Does the pitch level change?_____

Does the speaker use pauses effectively?_____

### PHYSICAL PRESENTATION:

Is his entire body involved in the delivery?_____ Does he use gestures?_____

Are there distracting mannerisms?_____

Is the posture good?_____ Does the speaker look alert?_____

Is there good facial expression?_____

# PREACH TO GET RESULTS

By Charles G. Finney

What is your motive when you preach? If you are aiming at increasing your own popularity--then, of course, your preaching will be suited for that purpose and not to convert souls to Christ!

Do you avoid preaching doctrines that are offensive to the carnal mind? Are you concerned your hearers might say to you--as they said to Christ--"This is a hard saying. Who can hear it?" Do you avoid making distinct points? Do you fear disturbing the consciences of your hearers, lest they become alarmed about their souls?

What about teaching techniques? Do you use good illustrations? Do you find interesting ways to repeat important statements? Do you emphasize the main points by your choice of words and by the tone of your voice? These devices will help people to remember what you say!

Do you strive to appeal mainly to the emotions of your hearers? You must strive to reach their consciences! Do you testify from your own personal experience of the power of the gospel? This will produce the conviction upon your hearers that you have something which they need.

Are you fearful about awakening in your hearers uncomfortable memories by reminding them of their unrepented sins? The Devil would have you denounce sin in general, but make no reference to the specific sins of your present audience! Don't yield to the Devil!

Weak preachers refrain from inviting their hearers to obey the truth here and now. But delayed obedience is disobedience! Be strong enough to present God's command and to gently press for immediate response. Expect them to commit themselves. Expect them to give their hearts to God, right on the spot! Do you instead leave the impression that they are expected to go away in their sins, and to consider the matter at their convenience? Is this the best way to preach for results?

Do you tell your people they are unable to obey? That they must wait for God to change them? Change will come after they commit their hearts and lives to Jesus! Lead them to accept Him now! It is good to preach that salvation is a gift from God. But be sure to point out that the sinners who are listening to you are condemned! They are lost! In this way they will understand what grace and salvation mean, and will see how much they need it! Preach the gospel as a remedy, but do not conceal or ignore the disease of the sinner which results in eternal death -- in Hell!

# ANSWERS TO SELF-TESTS

**CHAPTER ONE**:

1. Go ye therefore, and teach all nations, baptizing them in the name of the Father, and of the Son and of the Holy Ghost:

Teaching them to observe all things whatsoever I have commanded you: and, lo, I am with you alway, even unto the end of the world. (Matthew 28:19-20)

2. Matthew 28:18-19

3. The word "teach" means to instruct, show, demonstrate, inform, impart knowledge, train, and guide the studies of another. A "teacher" is one who teaches. "Teaching" is the act of instructing and training others.

4. We need teachers because they help explain God's Word to unbelievers [evangelism] and believers [discipleship]. Without teachers, people are like sheep without a shepherd.

5. The leadership position of "teacher" is one who leads and guides the church in addition to teaching. One with the speaking gift of teaching teaches, but does not hold a leadership position in the church.

6. The statement is true.

7. We are to teach all nations and faithful men who are able to teach others.

8. The two main objectives of teaching are evangelism and discipleship.

9. The three Biblical warnings discussed in this chapter are:

    -Teaching must be based on God's Word, not the doctrines of men.
    -Teachers must live what they teach.
    -There will be false teachers.

**CHAPTER TWO**:

1. The same came to Jesus by night, and said unto Him, Rabbi, we know that thou art a teacher come from God: for no man can do these miracles that thou doest, except God be with

Him. (John 3:2)

2. Compare your answer to the discussion in Chapter Two.

3. Compare your answer to the discussion in Chapter Two.

4. Compare your answer to the discussion in Chapter Two.

5. Jesus Christ.

6. Compare your answer to the discussion in Chapter Two.

7. Compare your answer to the discussion in Chapter Two.

8. Compare your answer to the discussion in Chapter Two.

9. John 20:21.

10. As the Father sent Jesus, so are we sent to accomplish similar purposes. His mission is our mission.

## CHAPTER THREE:

1. And as ye go, preach, saying, The Kingdom of Heaven is at hand.

Heal the sick, cleanse the lepers, raise the dead, cast out devils: freely ye have received, freely give. (Matthew 10:7-8)

2. The basic message of Jesus was all things pertaining to the Kingdom of God. This included how to enter the Kingdom [evangelism] and how to live as part of God's Kingdom [discipleship].

3. I Corinthians 15:1-4

4. The statement is True.

5. Power.

6. God's Word, the Holy Bible.

## CHAPTER FOUR:

There is no self-test for Chapter Four.

## CHAPTER FIVE:

1. And Jesus went about all the cities and villages, teaching in their synagogues, and preaching the gospel of the Kingdom, and healing every sickness and every disease among the people. (Matthew 9:35)

2-11. Compare your answers for these questions to the discussion of each subject in Chapter Five of this manual.

## CHAPTER SIX:

1. And when He was come into His own country, He taught them in their synagogue, insomuch that they were astonished, and said, Whence hath this man this wisdom, and these mighty works? (Matthew 13:54)

2-11. Compare your answers for these questions to the discussion of each subject in Chapter Six of this manual.

## CHAPTER SEVEN:

1. And He took a child, and set him in the midst of them: and when He had taken him in His arms, He said unto them,

Whosoever shall receive one of such children in my name, receiveth Me: and whosoever shall receive Me, receiveth not Me, but Him that sent Me. (Mark 9:36-37)

2. A teaching aid is something that aids you in teaching a lesson. It may be an activity which helps students understand a certain Biblical truth. It may also be an object which can be seen, heard, or touched [an audio-visual aid].

3. The word "audio" refers to hearing. The word "visual" refers to seeing. An "audio-visual aid" is something that can be seen and/or heard and which aids in learning.

4. Teaching aids are important because seeing, hearing, and doing are the main ways we learn.

5. He used simple objects from the environment.

## CHAPTER EIGHT:

1. But Jesus did not commit Himself unto them, because He knew all men. And needed not

that any should testify of man: for He knew what was in man. (John 2:24-25)

2. An "audience" is the group of people you will teach. To "analyze" something is to study it in detail, to carefully examine its characteristics, to study the parts of a whole. To analyze an audience means to carefully study the characteristics of a group of people you will teach.

3. Analyzing an audience is important because learning is affected by many factors such as language, education, culture, physical abilities, spiritual maturity, sex, marital status, social and economic level, personal needs, and age. If you do not analyze your audience you may be teaching above or below their educational and spiritual maturity levels. You may not use a language they understand. You may not relate your lessons to their social and economic level and to their personal needs.

4. Compare your summary to the discussion in Chapter Eight.

5. Compare your summary to that given for the age group you selected to write about.

**CHAPTER NINE**:

1. Whom we preach, warning every man, and teaching every man in all wisdom: that we may present every man perfect in Christ Jesus. (Colossians 1:28)

2. An objective is an aim or end of an action. It is a point, goal, or desired outcome to be achieved. When a teacher states objectives, he writes statements of goals for his students. These are stated to describe what the students will be able to do after completing the lesson.

3. -They direct the teacher's prayers, plans, teaching, and learning activities towards a specific goal.

-They can be used to measure the effectiveness of teaching.

-They improve your teaching.

-They help students become doers of the Word instead of only hearers.

4. General objectives are goals that apply to your teaching in general. They are objectives students should achieve over a period of time. Specific objectives differ from lesson to lesson. They are objectives specifically for an individual lesson.

5. Objective B is correct. It is stated in terms of observable student behavior.

6. The final goal of Biblical teaching is stated in Colossians 1:28.

## CHAPTER TEN:

1.  A wise teacher makes learning a joy. (Proverbs 15:2)

2.  Compare your list to the discussion in Chapter Ten.

3.
-Introduction
-Body
-Application
-Conclusion

4.  Compare your summary to the discussion in Chapter Ten.

5.  There is no right or wrong answer. The objective is that you are able to plan a lesson using the skills learned in this chapter.

## CHAPTER ELEVEN:

1.  That ye may approve things that are excellent; that ye may be sincere and without offence till the day of Christ. (Philippians 1:10)

2.  Evaluation is the process of carefully examining something.

3.  It is important that we carefully evaluate our teaching if we are to improve the gift God has given us.

4.
-Objectives
-Response
-Testing
-Teacher performance

5.  Compare your summary to the discussion in Chapter Eleven.

6.  You can use them as opportunities for spiritual growth and change. You can further develop your skill as a teacher.

## CHAPTER TWELVE:

1.  All Scripture is given by inspiration of God, and is profitable for doctrine, for reproof, for correction, for instruction in righteousness:

That the man of God may be perfect, thoroughly furnished unto all good works. (II Timothy 3:16-17)

2. The word "curriculum" refers to an organized course of study. It can refer to one course or all the courses used in a school. "Biblical curriculum" is an organized course of study of the Bible.

3. Compare your summary to the discussion in Chapter Twelve.

4. Use the skills learned in Chapter Ten of this course to develop a series of Bible lessons. Write these lessons out in detail. Eventually, you will have developed your own curriculum. Use the "Curriculum Evaluation Checklist" to help identify ways to improve the materials you develop.

## CHAPTER THIRTEEN:

1. The fear of the Lord is the beginning of wisdom: and the knowledge of the holy is understanding. (Proverbs 9:10)

2. An illiterate student is one who does not read or write his own language.

3. Compare your summary to the discussion in Chapter Thirteen.

## CHAPTER FOURTEEN:

1. For I have given unto them the words which thou gavest me; and they have received them, and have known surely that I came out from thee, and they have believed that thou didst send me. (John 17:8)

2. Pre-service training and in-service training.

3. Compare your summary to the discussion in Chapter Fourteen.

4. For recruitment suggestions see those listed in Chapter Fourteen.

5. Compare your summary to the discussion in Chapter Fourteen.

6. Compare your summary to the discussion in Chapter Fourteen.

7. You can evaluate a teacher:

-Using the skills learned in Chapter Eleven of this course.
-In terms of the ministry description.

-In relation to the keeping of the teacher's pledge.
-By observing them teach.
-By observing the "fruit" of their teaching.

## CHAPTER FIFTEEN:

1. How then shall they call on Him in whom they have not believed? and how shall they believe in Him of whom they have not heard? and how shall they hear without a preacher? And how shall they preach, except they be sent? (Romans 10:14-15a)

2. Preaching is the act of delivering a discourse [a sermon or systematic examination of a subject] which instructs others in a formal manner.

3. Compare your summary to the discussion in Chapter Fifteen.

4.

-Preachers must live what they preach.
-If you are specifically called preach, it is not an option.
-Preaching must be based on God's Word.
-Motives must be right.

5. Because the demonstration of God's power confirms the preaching of His Word.

## CHAPTER SIXTEEN:

1. Preach the word; be instant in season, out of season; reprove, rebuke, exhort with all longsuffering and doctrine. (II Timothy 4:2)

2. The basic differences between preaching and teaching are:

-The methods used in preaching often differ from those in teaching. Methods which call for audience participation are not commonly used because preaching usually involves a larger audience.

-The style of delivery differs in preaching because the audience usually includes all ages. The style of delivery must be adjusted to a common level that can be understood by children, youth, and adults.

-You usually do not have printed curriculum to guide as is often the case in Sunday school or church schools. With the direction of the Lord, you must determine the type and content of your message.

3. Basic steps for planning a sermon are like those of teaching. They include the following:

-Prepare yourself spiritually.
-Analyze the audience.
-Set objectives.
-Outline the message using the basic structure which includes an introduction, the body of the message, application, and the conclusion.

4. Topical preaching focuses on specific topics such as spiritual fruit, spiritual warfare, spiritual gifts, etc. You select a particular theme on one of these topics and develop it in the sermon.

5. In textual preaching, a key Biblical passage forms the central truth or text of the lesson. The remainder of the message is built on this one central truth.

6. Expository preaching is a more detailed type of preaching than topical or textual. It can focus on a specific subject or passage of Scripture, a book of the Bible, or a Bible character. It explains in detail all that is taught, verse by verse, and even word by word.

7. Compare your answer to the discussion in Chapter Sixteen.

8. Compare your answer to the discussion in Chapter Sixteen.

9. Compare your answer to the discussion in Chapter Sixteen.

CPSIA information can be obtained at www.ICGtesting.com
Printed in the USA
BVOW06s1722010914

364597BV00004B/11/P